The Classroom and Communication Skills Program

Practical Strategies for Educating Young Children with Autism Spectrum and Other Developmental Disabilities in the Public School Setting

Megan Ahlers, M. S., & Colleen Hannigan Zillich, M. S., CCC-SLP

Foreword by Cathy Pratt, Ph.D.

© 2008 Autism Asperger Publishing Co.
P.O. Box 23173
Shawnee Mission, Kansas 66283-0173
www.asperger.net • 913.897.1004

Publisher's Cataloging-in-Publication

Ahlers, Megan.
    The classroom and communication skills program : practical strategies for educating young children with autism spectrum and other developmental disabilities in the public school setting / Megan Ahlers & Colleen Hannigan Zillich. -- 1st ed. -- Shawnee Mission, Kan. : Autism Asperger Pub. Co., c2008.

        p. ; cm.
        ISBN: 978-1-934575-31-4
        LCCN: 2008935431
        Includes bibliographical references.

        1. Autistic children--Education. 2. Developmentally disabled children--Education. 3. Teachers of children with disabilities--Handbooks, manuals, etc. 4. Teaching--Aids and devices. I. Zillich, Colleen Hannigan. II. Title.

LC4717.8 .A45 2008   2008935431
371.94--dc22   0809

This book is designed in Myriad and CC Framistat.

Printed in the United States of America.

Cover photo: ©Shutterstock

Acknowledgments

We would like to thank our families, friends, and colleagues for their continued support and guidance. We would also like to thank our students and their families for their contributions to the Classroom and Communication Skills Program.

Table of Contents

While many early intervention books focus on more clinically based programs, *The Classroom and Communication Skills Program* provides a framework and detailed ideas on organizing and implementing a public school program. Topics address behavior, functional communication and play skills, relationship development, creating a classroom environment that supports students, sensory programming, and promoting parent-teacher partnerships.

Megan and Colleen also model how the energies and efforts of an educator and a speech clinician can be combined to create an instructional environment in which communication is embedded in every aspect of the classroom. Having seen firsthand their classroom, I am well aware of the challenges they faced and the successes they enjoyed. These are seasoned professionals who share their practical experiences and strategies, which have proven effective with a diverse range of students.

Readers will walk away from reading this book equipped with tools to reexamine and recreate their physical instructional environment and with ideas for specific activities. In addition, the authors provide a schedule for the day and explain how various times are used to teach specific skills. The chapter on assessment discusses the use of *The Assessment of Basic Language and Learning Skills* (ABLLS; Partington & Sundberg, 1998) in both identifying goal areas and in documenting progress. Other data collection systems are identified as well. The book ends with a chapter on frequently asked questions related to data collection, parent involvement, reinforcement identification, and time management.

I recommend this book to any teacher as a way to reassess and refocus various aspects of his or her public school program. For Megan and Colleen, the outcomes of their efforts were students who learned and made progress in every aspect of their lives. Hopefully, others will achieve the same outcomes as a result of implementing the recommendations in the book.

Cathy Pratt, Ph.D.
Director, Indiana Resource Center for Autism

We believe the least restrictive environment is a principle, not a place. The principle reflects the level of educational support necessary to implement effective programming. It is an idea that teaches us to look at the continuum of service or placement options for children. Early intervention refers to services for young children who have disabilities, developmental delays, or are at risk for developmental delays. Due to the recent rise in autism, a new program has been created to teach children functional and critical classroom and communication skills. The following is a vision of that program and the endless possibilities it embodies.

Our Three-Ring Circus

In the beginning, our classroom was composed of pre-school students with varying developmental needs. The majority of our students were verbal and able to independently engage in various activities. Early intervention was effective, and students made marked progress. Then one day, there was a knock on the door, and in came Jeremy.

Jeremy was an adorable 3-year-old held by his mother on his first day of school after transitioning from an early intervention program for infants and toddlers. Jeremy's mom handed him to us and we assured her that he was in good hands. Once his mom left and the door to the classroom was closed behind her, we put Jeremy down. As soon as his feet hit the floor, he was running. And we were running, too!

That first day and many days to follow were exhausting. Jeremy's favorite activities in the classroom included dancing on the table tops, climbing to the top of the bookcases, immersing himself in the sand table, and last but not least, free falling from the ledge of the white board. We were busy, and that was just one of our students. While we were trying to manage Jeremy's behavior, we were also teaching four students with special needs skills to transition to kindergarten – two 3-year-olds with mild language delays and one student who was nonverbal.

It soon became obvious that the design of our program would need to change so we could better meet the needs of all of our students. Not knowing where to start, we began grouping the students according to their abilities and needs, thus creating three separate groups. Hence, our three-ring circus! In ring one, we were teaching the children their ABCs and other prekindergarten readiness skills. In ring two, we were focusing on teaching

TIP: A child is not able to "work" with you if he does not like being with you.

basic concepts and grammar. And ring three, we were teaching the children how to request their basic wants and needs. In our best attempt to group the students for academic progress, we were really just doing "damage control" to make sure that everyone made it through the day alive! We felt as if we were spinning our wheels but going nowhere.

It was an exhausting time, and we later figured out that we were missing many signals our children were sending us on how to restructure their school day to be both functional and fun. During the spring of that same year, we received training in applied behavioral analysis and applied verbal behavior (Skinner, 1957). Prior to the workshop, we felt like we were on a sinking ship, but the knowledge from this inservice gave us something to hold on to so we could begin to teach Jeremy more effectively.

Jeremy's Influence on Our Classroom

After Jeremy's arrival in our classroom, we stepped back from our current practices and realigned our teaching approach to better meet his needs. The first step was to build a positive relationship with this child. We began to follow his lead by observing his interests and noting what he found motivating. By dropping our own agenda, we were able to gain insight into how to teach this child.

The sand table was a highly preferred activity for Jeremy. Instead of fighting the uphill battle of constantly redirecting him to sit in the chair (to prevent him from climbing into the sand table), we used sand to our advantage as a motivator. We filled a shallow plastic bin with sand and placed it under a classroom chair. By incorporating a reinforcing item into an activity, we motivated Jeremy to sit independently. Suddenly he did not find sitting in a chair at the table so bad as long as he could place his bare feet into the sand.

The Power of Receipts

Active engagement is an all-important goal. If the child is not engaged, you need to question whether he is learning. Our students seemed to be experts in task-avoidance behavior. Children who prefer to be alone or who perseverate on objects/routines rather than joining others in classroom activities are a challenge. The key is to determine, on a moment-by-moment basis, what are motivating reinforcers for each child.

Early in the development of the program, we primarily used small/mini-food items, including fruit snacks and candy, as reinforcers. They could be given out in small amounts, and we did not have to deal with the issue of having to take them back because they were quickly consumed. Non-edible reinforcing items, on the other hand, such as a favorite toy had a tendency to create a power struggle when we needed to take the item away in exchange for the task at hand. However, it wasn't long before dietary restrictions and experience moved us to consider other reinforcing items beyond food. (Chapter 2 provides more information on how to use motivating items to shape behaviors.)

TIP: Incorporate a child's interest into activities to promote participation.

To determine reinforcing items for each child, we observed the child in the classroom, consulted with parents, and made home visits to determine the child's strong interests.

During a home visit, one of our students, CJ, kept laughing and running back and forth holding a grocery store receipt. Mom informed us that the more numbers it listed and the longer the receipt, the happier CJ was. Without this home visit, we would never have discovered the power of receipts! From then on, we were able to use receipts in the classroom to help motivate CJ to participate in activities.

TIP: Always think outside the box! Reinforcers can take any shape or form, depending on the child's preferences.

Developing a Parent-Teacher Team

To develop an effective program for children with autism and other developmental disabilities, a parent-teacher partnership is critical. We held evening workshops to offer parents information on communication skills, behavior management strategies, as well as understanding the development of play. The workshop topics were designed to support parents in addressing their child's development and interests at home.

In addition to parent-teacher workshops, student home visits were important components of the program. Here we were able

TIP: *Seek out the parents and encourage them to be active partners in their child's education.*

to see the children in their natural environment, observe skills they demonstrated at home, get new ideas for reinforcers, as well as bridge the home environment with the school environment. This created a fluid transition between the child's primary natural environments of home and school. Building relationships with each parent promoted collaboration. Not surprisingly, we found that parents were the keepers of a wealth of information about their child.

Assessment Tools

When Jeremy began our program, we found that the assessment tools we had been using were insufficient to give us a clear picture of his present level of performance. In searching for a tool that would identify Jeremy's skills so we could build upon them, we found the *Assessment of Basic Language and Learning Skills* (ABLLS; Partington & Sundberg, 1998). This instrument gave us important insight into the child's fundamental skills. (Chapter 6 provides additional information on assessments.)

Creating the Classroom and Communication Skills Program

As an outcome of trying to rescue our sinking ship, we combined all these elements to create a new public school program for early childhood students – The Classroom and Communication Skills Program (CCSP). The CCSP not only addresses the educational needs of Jeremy but of all students who have significant communication and classroom challenges.

TIP: *An effective assessment is one that tells you what the child can do.*

The Long and Winding Road ...

The road seemed very long and tiring, but it was evident early on that this would be a gratifying and rejuvenating journey. In the chapters to follow, you will find a practical, systematic approach to creating your own CCSP for children with autism and other developmental disabilities.

The Classroom and Communication Skills Program - Overview

Our vision for the Classroom and Communication Skills Program (CCSP) was to create a classroom in a public school setting that targeted basic foundational communication and classroom skills. The program is designed for children who are nonverbal and who have difficulties engaging in and attending to typical classroom activities. Specifically, we wanted to provide multiple opportunities for the children to learn to:

- request,
- demonstrate joint attention, and
- engage in functional play and adult-directed activities.

The following is an overview of our classroom and how we structured the day to meet the needs of our students.

Students

Children are recommended for the CCSP based upon their classroom performance and communication skills. Because of its special design, the program lends itself to the needs of children with autism and other developmental disabilities, including Down syndrome, cerebral palsy, and traumatic brain injuries. The children attend four half days per week for a total of 12 hours of instruction (3 hours per day). Each child is registered for either a morning or an afternoon session. We typically have six students in each session.

Staff

The daily staff of the CCSP consists of an early childhood special education teacher and an instructional assistant. In addition, a speech therapist provides speech and language services to the

TIP: Throughout this book, you will see examples of how we have used Boardmaker Software by Mayer-Johnson (www.Mayer-Johnson.com). Boardmaker offers three software products that cover a broad range of communication and special education needs. Other picture symbols may also be used or you can draw your own.

children directly in their classroom setting two full days per week. An occupational therapist provides services in the class-room one day per week, based upon the length of time recom-mended in each child's individualized education program (IEP). If the child requires physical therapy, the physical therapist joins the class on the playground or provides therapy in a separate area with specialized equipment (e.g., balance beam, stairs).

All related services are integrated into the natural environment of the classroom. This arrangement assists the children with generalization of skills and also allows the therapists to follow the child's lead, teach in the moment, and model strategies for other staff members.

Students attend class Monday through Thursday. On Fridays, the teaching staff prepare materials, hold case conferences, make home visits, and participate in trainings and collaborative plan-ning. By having the speech therapist and classroom teacher plan together, integrated classroom materials are available for use throughout the week. Materials are created to encourage children's independence skills, promote functional communica-tion, teach pre-academics, and support them with transitions between activities within the classroom.

Schedule Boards and Transitions

Schedule boards – visual representations of the daily schedule – are typically created with pictures, but objects, photos, and written language may also be used. Visual schedules teach the child the sequence of events and by doing so help reduce anxiety connected with having to make transitions. Once the child understands how to use her visual schedule, she is better able to function independently.

How to Create a Visual Schedule
Schedule boards are typically made on thick cardboard, foam board, or binders. They can be portable or mounted to surfaces such as the wall, door, or refrigerator.
To make a visual schedule, you will need picture/object rep-resentation of activity, adhering material or magnets, and mounting material.

Even though visual schedules are great tools to help students transition between activities, for many children, a schedule of the whole day is too overwhelming. If this is the case, break the schedule into discrete steps. Teach each step and then build upon the child's success. Our recommendation is to begin teaching the visual schedule with an activity that the child enjoys (e.g., snack).

TIP: *To support a child's transitions, provide visual supports and an effective reinforcer.*

Teaching Children How to Use Their Schedule Boards

First, the child must want to go to the different area/activity on the schedule. To encourage the child to successfully transition to the new location, we place favorite items on/at the designated areas.

Second, the pictures on the picture schedule must hold meaning for the child. The child is taught matching skills and that each picture represents a location or activity.

Each child is given his own portable schedule board, which includes a photograph of the child and a single picture representing the next activity.

An adult holds a larger picture of the activity or points to the picture on the wall. The children transition between activities by matching their small activity picture to a larger picture in the corresponding location.

The adult in the final destination has a variety of reinforcers to encourage the children to transition independently. As the children become proficient at using their simplified visual schedule, pictures are added as gradual steps toward creating a full individualized schedule board.

Jeremy's individual schedule board and corresponding location picture.

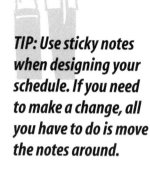

TIP: Use sticky notes when designing your schedule. If you need to make a change, all you have to do is move the notes around.

Classroom Schedule and Activities

In addition to individual student schedules, daily classroom schedules are created for the adults so they know who is responsible for which child during activities. For example, on Wednesdays, the red dot next to an activity/name means the teacher is responsible; the blue dot means the instructional assistant is responsible; and the yellow dot means that both are required to support the child.

As illustrated below, the daily schedule is broken into 15-minute increments. This helps ensure maximum attention and focus for both the adults and students during instructional sessions. Daily schedules are created to display the expected routine and are reflective of specials, activities, and therapies. For example, on Tuesdays and Thursdays, the speech language pathologist supports the classroom. Having this additional support creates more opportunities for one-on-one instructional time in the classroom.

The classroom daily schedule is organized into different components to maximize a child's communication and classroom foundation skills. Specifically, communication skills are composed of the child's language output using words, pictures, manual signs, gestures, and/or assistive technology and the child's understanding of language. (See Chapter 3 for more information on communication.) Classroom foundation skills refer to the child's ability to sit and engage in adult- and child-directed activities. (See Chapter 2 for more information on classroom foundational skills and behavior.)

The example of a daily classroom schedule on page 9 will be further detailed.

Sample classroom schedule for the adults.

Daily A.M. Classroom Schedule	
8:30-8:35 a.m.	Arrival
8:35-8:40 a.m.	Hanging up coats and backpacks in the classroom
8:40-8:45 a.m.	Play time
8:45-9:00 a.m.	Circle time
9:00-9:15 a.m.	Gross-motor activities
9:15-9:30 a.m.	First small-group session
9:30-9:45 a.m.	Second small-group session
9:45-10:00 a.m.	Circle time
10:00-10:30 a.m.	Snack time
10:30-11:00 a.m.	Bathroom (occurring simultaneously with third and fourth small-group sessions)
10:30-10:45 a.m.	Third small-group session
10:45-11:00 a.m.	Fourth small-group session
11:00-11:20 a.m.	Large-group activity
11:15-11:30 a.m.	Dismissal

The classroom schedule offers structure for the classroom program. Lesson plans, driven by the child's needs, are created to fit within the scheduled events. As such, the classroom schedule is the framework for how you envision the day will unfold; however, be flexible to allow for the individual adjustment of implementation.

The Comprehensive Autism Planning System (CAPS) for Individuals with Asperger Syndrome, Autism, and Related Disabilities: Integrating Best Practices Throughout the Student's Day by Shawn Henry and Brenda Smith Myles (2007) is an excellent resource to help the educational team identify how, as well as when, to implement the instruction. See the example on page 10.

Comprehensive Autism Planning System (CAPS)

Child/Student: ___Ginny___

*ss=state standard

Time	Activity	Targeted Skills to Teach	Structure/ Modifications	Reinforcement	Sensory Strategies	Communication/ Social Skills	Data Collection	Generalization Plan
7:30-7:55	Breakfast	Choose breakfast using breakfast board Using interactive language board Independent schedule use	Choice board of breakfast items Interactive language board Visual schedule	Choice of food items	Not at this time	Have additional social language on board (i.e., greetings, questions) Work on table manners	Data sheet for choice Data on use of language board	Use language board during lunch or dinner at home
8:05-8:20	Independent morning work Lunch count prep	Independent work of mastered math problems Self-monitoring Review menu for lunch choices Charting lunch count Collect and organize data (ss) Follow two- and three-step oral directions (ss)	Visuals to break down task (1-5, raise hand, finished) Visual focusing aid Visual schedule Priming for lunch count Trained peer buddy	Complete 5 problems – get a break of her choice Social reinforcement from peers	Ginny needs black construction paper box around problem to write in box Slant board with textured paper underneath for more feedback Sticky string for lunch graphing sheet	Follow general education classroom rules Review lunch choices Ginny will ask peers if they have one of the lunch choices by holding the choice up and saying the name (i.e., hamburger, sack lunch) Interpersonal skills (proximity to peer)	Use of self-monitoring sheets, % independent Data sheet for transitions	Self-monitoring in other subjects Using peers' names throughout the school day
8:20-9:00	1) Attendance 2) Lunch count 3) Morning work 4) Calendar	Collect and organize data (ss) Names of classmates Reciprocal interaction with peers Self-monitoring Using language board for calendar skills Measure calendar time (ss) List days and months in order (ss)	Systematic prompting (least-most) for use of language board Task analysis of morning work using pictures (she will put in finished slot when completed) Visual schedule	Social reinforcement from peers	Sensory items available (lotion, koosh ball) Change positions if lying on desk Slant board	PECS book Language board for lunch count Language board for calendar activities Interpersonal skills (proximity to peer)	Copy attendance from board Language board use (+ if she uses board, * if she uses board and verbalizes) Data sheet for transitions	Using classmates' names in hall, playground, lunch, etc.
9:00-9:30	SPECIALS M Computer T Library W TH Video	Using language board – increase MLU Follow two- and three-step oral directions (ss) Independent use of schedule for transitions	Trained peer buddies Modified rules to game to increase communication Visual schedule Mini-schedule (task analysis)	Game playing Movement Social reinforcement from peers	Smaller and controlled setting	Reciprocal interaction with peers Increasing MLU through use of language board Turn taking Cooperative learning groups	Data sheet for transitions Data on use of language board	Use language boards during lunch and dinner at home
9:35-10:00	Whole-group Reading Spelling Writing	Print legibly (ss) Use active listening strategies (ss) Establish purpose for reading (ss)	Visual schedule Visuals accompanying text General visual support from common items needed in class Games to go along with text	Game playing Movement	Built-in physical activity (i.e., fishing game)	Reading or game with peer	Data sheet for transitions	

Visual Time Timer® by Time Timer, LLC.

Now, let's look in more detail at the various activities of the day.

8:30-8:35 a.m. – Arrival

Under adult supervision, as the children arrive in the morning, they are instructed to sit on the floor in the hallway until all of their peers have arrived. This is an excellent opportunity to teach the children to sit and wait. If a child needs a visual cue to wait, teach him to hold a pre-made "wait" card or use a visual timer so he knows how much longer he has to wait.

Once the children arrive, we give them the direction to sit down, using reinforcers, words, manual signs, and/or a picture. As soon as the child sits, he receives a favorite item. If he gets up, we take away the item, request that he sit down, and then return the desired item once he is seated. (Chapter 2 will further explain how to use reinforcers effectively.) The following example illustrates how to encourage a child to sit and wait for the entire group to assemble.

Complete Visual Support Set (2004) from Pyramid Educational Products, Inc.

As soon as Grace entered the school building, she took off running down the hall. Knowing she was reinforced by all things pretty, to replace the running behavior with appropriate sitting and waiting, we showed her nail polish as she came into the building. By showing her the item, pointing to the floor, and then requesting her to sit, we were able to make Grace comply with the request to sit down in the hallway. Immediately upon her sitting, we put glittery nail polish on one of her finger nails.

Of course, this did not keep her seated for the entire wait time (about 5 minutes), so when she became fidgety, one of us would say, "I have nail polish. You need to sit down." This reminder encouraged her to sit as we painted another nail. Grace's reinforcers changed frequently throughout her day. One minute nail polish would work, next a sticker, a bracelet, or even a foot bath would be effective. It is important to vary reinforcers to maximize their value.

When using reinforcers, remember that the same item does not work all the time. For example, if you love chocolate, the power of doing something for chocolate will decrease if you are given chocolate all day long. Vary the reinforcers and look for new items to expand the range of the child's reinforcers. In our classroom, John loved markers he could roll in his hands. To expand his reinforcers, we collected other items

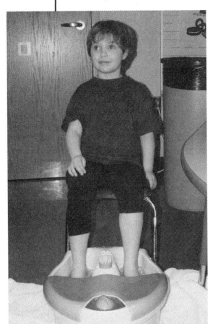

Grace waiting appropriately with her feet in a footbath. She is also learning to verbally request "turn on!"

he could roll with his hands, including cylindrical blocks, pencils, and straws. This helped to increase the number of motivating reinforcers and decrease the burnout rate of always using markers.

8:35-8:40 a.m. – Hanging up Backpacks and Coats

Once all the children have arrived, we walk to the classroom and encourage them to hang up their coats and backpacks. Each child's cubby is labeled with his or her picture and name. As the child is asked to hang up her backpack, the adult also presents the manual sign for "backpack" and a picture of a backpack. That is, multiple modalities of presenting directions are used to encourage the child's independent success in performing the task.

8:40-8:45 a.m. – Play Time

During the first few minutes of the classroom day, the children are able to explore the environment and play with different toys and materials. The classroom environment is prearranged, by the teacher strategically placing toys and materials in the front of the room. Daily play items include cars, shape sorters, books, balls, doll houses, farm animals, and puzzles. The children are encouraged to move freely between play areas. This environment allows the children to individualize the ways in which they experience the content in a self-directed learning activity, with the teacher taking on the role of a facilitator. That is, the adult follows the child's lead.

TIP: Corral children near their cubbies by moving your body back and forth to stay behind the children to avoid creating an open space for them to run away from the area. Redirect the child by pointing to the activity at hand.

Dylan approaching a toy at the table.

Many of the toys are set out on table tops. As the child approaches and then engages in play with a toy, an adult carefully offers the child a chair to sit in. The adult compliments the child's sitting skills and pulls up a chair for herself to sit in next to the child. The toys and activities are used to promote language and play skills as well as to serve as possible reinforcers to help the child comply during activities. Rotate toys each week and limit the number of choices. This will help expand the child's repertoire of play and make the environment less stimulating to avoid overstimulation.

To transition to circle time, we sing a song and the children are given their portable schedule boards. Some of the children walk independently to their chairs while others require a reinforcer (usually the toy the child was playing with during play time) to transition.

8:45-9:00 a.m. – Circle Time

Once they have transitioned, the children sit independently in cube chairs, which gives them boundaries; some with, and others without reinforcers.

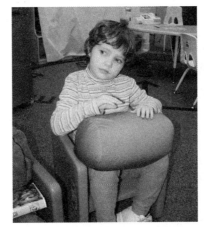

Students sitting in cube chairs at circle time with reinforcers.

Circle starts with our "hello" song. The children are encouraged through the use of reinforcers to imitate the various movements and words during this routine song. Following the song, the children take turns placing their own photograph on a school house. This activity targets each child's self-identification, following one-step directions, and complying with our finger point to place the picture in a specific location.

Next the children each have an opportunity to pick a song. Pictures representing each song choice are posted on a large board from which the teacher can easily pull song choices and place them onto a smaller board for each child. Some of the children eventually become able to choose a song by using the large board.

Depending on the child's discrimination ability, one to three song choices from the song choice board are offered, including one of his favorite songs.

> **Note:** *Some song choices are specifically included because they have a calming effect on the students and serve to deescalate adverse behaviors. Calming songs include "Wonderful World" by Rod Stewart and "Brown Bear, Brown Bear, What Do You See?" by Greg and Steve.*

As the children each take a turn, they are encouraged to remove the picture of their song choice from the board and hand it to the teacher. The teacher then moves the song choices to different lo-

TIP: Limit the use of seat-belted chairs. This type of chair does not teach the child to sit independently. In place of seat belts, use reinforcers to encourage the child to sit during an activity. When the child gets out of his chair, take the reinforcer back and then redirect the child to sit in the chair. Once the child sits, immediately redeliver the reinforcer. If the child is not responding to the request, you may need to select a different reinforcer that will be motivating.

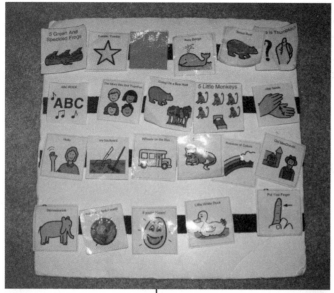

(Top) Song choice board includes all possible song choices.
(Bottom) Individual song choice board.

TIP: Pause favorite songs before repetitive lines to see if the children are able to fill in the blank using a sound, word, or manual sign. Encourage the children to point to different pictures in the song books to increase their understanding of the words and to promote pointing skills.

cations on the individual choice board to prevent the child from choosing a song solely based on its location. The child is then asked to find the song he previously requested. This helps the child to consistently and reliably request using pictures. Finally, the picture song choice is shown to the students as the song plays to increase association between the picture and the song.

The songs sung during circle time are used to teach language, imitation, as well as academic and social skills. During the songs, the adults sing and produce manual signs and use various visual aids to communicate the songs in a multi-sensory format. Song books are also created using Mayer-Johnson Boardmaker® and Microsoft Publisher® to provide visuals and to increase the child's engagement and attending skills.

"Wonderful World" song book created on Microsoft Publisher ® using Boardmaker ® pictures and clip art photographs. This book served as a visual support for engagement while singing this song.

Props are also used during songs to increase the child's understanding of the concepts presented, to promote generalization, and to increase active engagement.

To promote generalization, we use a variety of items during songs – pictures, actual objects, and toys. Engagement, joint attention, sitting skills, and imitation are the focus of circle time.

During circle time, we incorporate a thematic-based book and activity. We have found that many children's books are either too distracting or too wordy for our students. So, we have taken the framework of those books and modified them to be more appropriate for our students or created completely new books using Boardmaker® and Microsoft Publisher®.

We have added pictures, simplified the text, created a repetitive line, and integrated actual objects into our stories. We use these books throughout the week to promote the learning of targeted concepts, matching skills, identifying and labeling vocabulary, and pointing to pictures.

Page 16 shows sample pages from a book we created about penguins. The concepts of "in" and "out" were targeted. The children participated by tossing a rubber penguin *in* a bucket of water and taking it *out* of the bucket again.

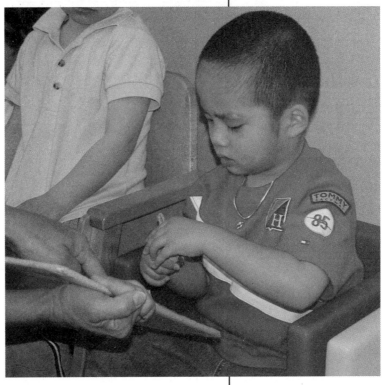

(Top) "Wheels on the Bus" song props.

(Bottom) John placing the horn on the bus during "The Wheels on the Bus" song. The targeted skill was for John to independently take the item from the teacher and put it "on" the board.

TIP: Include fill-ins throughout the day. The child can fill in the blank using any communication modality, including words, manual signs, sounds, pictures, voice output devices, and/or gestures.

Penguins

In   and   Out

of the Water

Out of the Water

In the Water

The following are sample pages from other books we created for use in the classroom.

At the end of circle time, the teacher plays the closing song. This is the same song each day and signals to the children that circle time is ending. Once the song is over, the teacher says and signs "Circle time is all done; circle time is all … done." By pausing at the end of the second phrase, we encourage the children to fill in the last word. The children then transition to a gross-motor activity using their individualized schedules (see page 7).

9:00-9:15 a.m. – Gross-Motor Activity

Gross-motor activities include inside or outside physical play. Regardless of location, the children are encouraged to explore their environment, play appropriately with materials, and request actions and objects.

Outside Play

Outside play is an opportunity for the children to interact socially with peers. At the same time, requesting and play skills are taught. For example, instead of just pushing the child on the swing, we prompt her to request to swing using words, manual signs, and/or pictures. Fill-ins are used while the children access various pieces of equipment (e.g., "Ready, set … go!").

We also model play skills that are new for the children. For example, we sit and swing on the swings next to or with the child, teaching him how to pump his legs to create motion. If students need assistance to slide down the slide, we place them on our laps and slide down together.

Outdoor time is not limited to the playground equipment. We also teach the children how to dig in the ground, fill buckets with wa-

A pig likes to play in the mud.

A pig plays in the...**mud**!

I see trees of green, red roses too
I see them bloom for me and you

(Top) Sample page from the farm book we created to teach the children to imitate the final word of a phrase (i.e., fill-ins).

(Bottom) Sample page from the "Wonderful World" songbook we created to teach visual representation.

ter, push large toy cars, and chase after each other! For children who do not enjoy the outside environment, favorite items are taken onto the playground to help increase their tolerance.

Ben and Grace playing appropriately on the playground.

Indoor Play

During indoor gross-motor activities, the children engage with sensory items, including water, sand, and shaving cream, as well as gross-motor equipment, such as a small exercise trampoline, a small plastic slide, exercise balls, a swing, a ball pit, and plastic rocking animals.

Children with autism spectrum disorders have sensory needs throughout the day. In place of sensory breaks, we integrate sensory opportunities into daily activities. For example, for students who like to watch things spin, a water wheel is placed in the water bin to promote play. For the child who likes movie character figurines, figurines are placed in the sand table.

Danny playing with the water wheel in a plastic storage bin slightly filled with water.

During these activities, fill-ins such as "Ready, set ... *go*!,""up and ... *down*" and "one, two ... *three*" are targeted. Students are shown models of how to use pictures and manual signs for fill-ins. Gross-motor activities also target requesting and joint attention skills. The following scenario describes how we taught a child to use the indoor slide appropriately.

During indoor gross-motor time, Emma would climb up the ladder of our small plastic slide. Once at the top, she attempted to free fall to the floor. To replace this behavior, we used a reinforcer and various prompts to encourage her to sit down and go down the slide. Once

John in the ball pit following a one-step direction to give us a ball.

Emma sat down, she was given her favorite toy and guided down the slide. We were able to teach her how to safely play on a slide through the use of a reinforcer and prompts.

Providing sensory-based items along with effective reinforcers reduced the need for sensory breaks away from activities. Please see Chapter 2 for additional ideas of how to integrate sensory activities into the child's school day.

CJ jumping on the trampoline after requesting to jump using a visual card.

9:15-9:30 a.m.; 9:30-9:45 a.m. – Small-Group Sessions

Small-group sessions are designed to facilitate development in the cognitive domain by targeting concepts the child has not yet mastered, offering immediate assessment, as well as giving the child practice in application of the concepts. Curriculum instruction and art are offered during small-group sessions.

Curriculum Instruction

The children practice various language and academic skills such as requesting, following directions, naming and identifying vocabulary, pointing, and matching. The content and process for responding is individualized as the teacher gives direct instruction and/or uses visuals in a rapid fashion. The following are sample activities used during curriculum instruction.

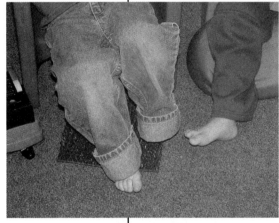

Children's feet on a piece of artificial turf mat for sensory input during an activity.

Puzzles

Instead of having the children attempt to complete single inset puzzles independently, the adult presents each child with a choice of two puzzle pieces. This addresses choice making, naming vocabulary, and pointing. The adult also asks the child to find a specific piece, which addresses following directions and identifying vocabulary.

TIP: Provide sensory input when the child needs it, not just when it is listed on the schedule.

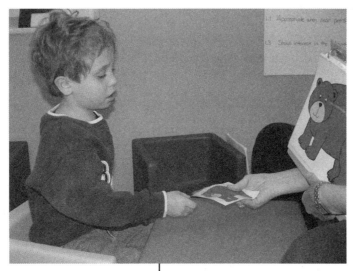

CJ matching picture to picture using Brown Bear, Brown Bear visuals (Martin, 1970).

Matching Pictures and Objects

The teacher places a set of pictures or objects in a divider tray. To begin, the child is asked to match a single object or picture. The field increases as the child's skills progress. If the child struggles to match independently, the adult models the correct match and then represents the task for the child to complete.

Shape Sorter

Shape sorters are used to teach visual discrimination skills. To begin, present the child with shape sorter pieces one at a time. Typically, children (a) put the shape in by visually locating the correct location, (b) put the shape in by trial and error, or (c) are not able to place shapes. For the child in Group A, more difficult shape sorters are introduced. For the child in Group B, the adult adds a gestural prompt of a point to the correct location. Finally, for the child in Group C, two out of the three possible placements are covered to promote errorless learning where the child cannot fail at a task. By using errorless learning, the child is successful in manipulating the materials. As the child becomes more proficient, this prompt is faded and replaced with a less invasive prompt, such as a gestural cue. During all of these scenarios, basic concepts of "in" and "out" are targeted.

Ball drop

Musical ball-drop toys not only teach visual discrimination and tracking skills but also cause-and-effect and functional play skills. By using a toy such as a musical ball drop, which creates a cause-and-effect reaction, the child attends

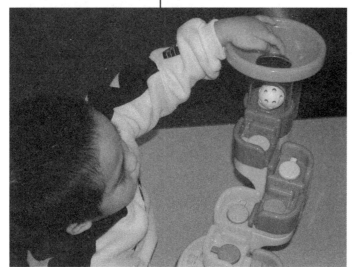

John placing the ball in the ball drop toy independently.

beyond the time it takes to drop the ball in the hole. The action of dropping the ball into the top of the toy might need to be modeled along with providing a reinforcer to complete the task. Initially, the children might also need gestural prompts to follow the direction to "put the ball in." Eventually, by fading the prompts, students become able to independently play with this highly motivating toy.

Art

The focus of art is on the process, not the product. A child can be taught positional concepts (e.g., on/off, up/down), common vocabulary (e.g., paint, paper, water), thematic vocabulary (e.g., animal names, clothing, vehicles), fine-motor skills (e.g., squeezing, pincher grasp), and so much more, through art activities.

When planning art projects, always think about what you want the children to learn. In addition, think about how to teach children what to do with different art supplies. For example, they may not understand that a paintbrush is for painting. They may think it is for chewing or for tossing across the room. Show children what to do – don't assume they know.

Children can be art lovers or art avoiders. The art lovers come to the art table with minimal prompting. Once at the table, the activity itself often serves as a reinforcer. However, these students also try to put various art supplies in their mouth, including glue, paint, chalk, markers, and paper. To encourage appropriate use of art materials, remember to take baby steps. For example, if the child tries to eat the paint, place a small amount of paint on the paper first and encourage the child to make brush strokes. As the child's engagement increases with the activity, continue to add the progressive steps to reach your goal for the child. Remember children learn through exploring – encourage the process over the product and allow the child to get messy.

The art avoiders, on the other hand, will do everything possible to get away from the activity, including crying when a drop of paint or glue touches their hands. For these students, we also use baby steps to get them to complete art tasks. For example, CJ would not

> **TIP:** Often students don't know how to engage in appropriate play with toys. Instead of playing with them functionally, they fixate on one specific element, such as watching the wheels of a car spin instead of pushing the car. Incorporate reinforcers to support play development and imitation of motor movements with toys. Invest in a variety of cause-and-effect toys to promote functional play. Also, provide two sets of identical or similar toys so you can model various actions alongside the child.

Jeremy completing his art project with the reinforcer of a peg board visible. This art activity targeted squeezing glue and matching colored dinosaurs.

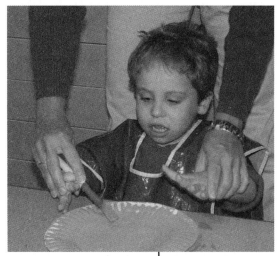

Painting skills in the fall: CJ needed support to hold the paintbrush.

Painting skills the following spring: CJ painted independently. The doll (top right of the picture) served as his reinforcer to complete the project.

touch a paintbrush. When the brush was placed in his hand, he arched his back and bit his hand. Our ultimate goal was for him to paint on paper with a paintbrush. However, our first goal was for him to touch the paintbrush.

We knew that CJ loved figurines from his favorite movie. We capitalized on this by pairing characters with touching the paintbrush. If he touched the paintbrush, he was reinforced with a figurine. Later demands included CJ picking up the paintbrush, touching the paintbrush to the paper, dipping the paintbrush in the paint, and finally painting independently. By taking these gradual steps, he was able to paint independently by the end of the school year.

Limit the amount of hand-over-hand assistance given during art. A child may need this initially, but fade this prompt quickly. Even if the child needs physical prompts, determine a task within the activity that he can complete independently. For example, the child may touch the paintbrush, put the paintbrush into the sink, or squeeze the glue independently.

If a child is always physically prompted, he will learn to wait for your assistance to complete a task. This is referred to as being prompt-dependent. Instead of physical prompting, use a combination of models, reinforcers, gestural prompts, picture prompts, and verbal prompts to initially teach the child. Fade these prompts to get to the ultimate goal of independence.

9:45-10:00 a.m. – Circle Time

Circle time in the middle of the day is designed to reinforce concepts taught in the earlier circle time and to introduce new songs and activities. This second circle time also provides additional opportunities for all students to request desired songs (some days we don't have enough time to have each child request during the first circle time).

When a new song is introduced, the adult shows the picture that matches the song. This teaches the children which picture represents the new song. After multiple presentations, the children relate the picture to the song and are then given the picture as a song choice.

10:00-10:30 a.m. – Snack Time

Prior to snack time, an adult sets up the snacks and places the student pictures and visuals down on the table. The children transition from circle to snack time using their individual schedule boards (see page 7). Use of the individual schedule is usually successful during this time because the children are motivated to transition to snack time. The children sit at a U-shaped snack table next to their pictures. Student placement at the table is rotated on a daily basis to avoid dependence on sitting in the same spot.

Organization and preparation are essential. Create lesson plans and select snacks in advance. During preparation times, the pictures of snack choices are organized into individual student envelopes, making it easy to set up snack quickly. To support children's dietary restrictions, snack choices are placed in a divided tray to keep gluten-casein foods separate from other foods. The divided tray also increases the ease in which the adult can access the food items. Pictures (line drawings or digital pictures) of each child's individual snacks are laminated and placed on a Velcro® strip or on a menu board.

The number of snack choices varies for each child. If a child is learning to request, a single picture of a desired food item is placed on the table. As the child becomes proficient, choices are added to the menu.

Snack time provides excellent opportunities to target functional requests. The children are taught to request using pictures, sign language, spoken language, and assistive technology. (Chapter 3 provides additional information on using this total communication approach.)

TIP: Store additional copies of pictures alphabetically in a drawer near snack. Pictures are frequently chewed or ripped, so it is necessary to have replacements.

TIP: Add nonpreferred items to a child's menu to ensure the child is discriminating between presented choices. If a child's choices are all things he loves, why would he need to actually look at the pictures? When non-preferred choices are incoporated, the child is more easily taught the meaning of each individual picture.

After the child requests a snack item, the adult gives him a very small quantity (e.g., a quarter of a cookie, two small fruit snacks) to promote additional requests – if we gave the child his entire snack after only one request, we would be missing numerous teaching opportunities.

Ben producing the manual sign and beginning sound for "fish" to request a fish cracker.

Some children only eat a snack if given the whole snack item. For example, Mike would scream when he was given a broken cookie but was ecstatic with a whole cookie. To increase his number of requests, we gave him the entire cookie but took it back after he took a bite.

During snack, "more" is not used as a request. This is a generic request that does not indicate a child's specific wants. If the child is only taught to request "more," the adults will not know what he wants "more" of, leading to frustration. Instead, we provide pictures of the child's favorite items and model these manual signs.

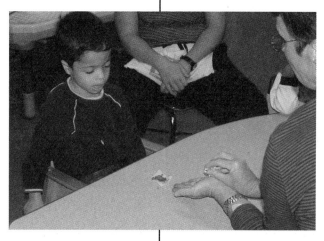

Danny learning to request French fries with a single picture exchange.

Again, limit the amount of hand-over-hand assistance provided. Some children inadvertently learn to put out their hands for the adults to manipulate to request. Avoid this by using modeling to encourage independent responses. You may need to use physical prompts when a child is learning a new skill. If the child is learning to request with pictures, tap his elbow to prompt him to grab the picture as opposed to taking his hand and placing it on the picture. This encourages the child to be more independent. If a child is learning manual signs, tap his hands and model the sign instead of always manipulating his hands to make the signs.

Just as a child learning to speak does not say words perfectly at first, a child learning to use manual signs will first make approximations and then refine the signs as she becomes more proficient. When prompting a child, always think about how you can fade your prompts to promote independence and avoid prompt dependency.

If a child is not eating at school, consult with the parents and, if necessary, make a home visit during mealtime. Children with autism spectrum disorders can be very specific about what they will eat based upon how it is presented. By utilizing successful strategies and items from home, you may be able to generalize eating to school. This may include offering a specific plate, cup, utensil, or brand of food to bridge eating from home to school.

Students requesting desired items at the snack table. Turn taking and waiting skills are also taught during this time.

Our student, John, refused to eat at school (pictured at right with a reinforcing toy at the snack table). However, he was still expected to sit at the snack table with a toy. We continued to present him with snack choices. On a field trip, we observed John eating crackers out of a teddy bear-shaped container. We were surprised and asked his parents to send in the container. Sure enough, John began to eat at school when we used the bear container.

10:30-11:00 a.m. – Bathroom Rotation

Each child is individually taken to the bathroom on a rotation basis. Rotation allows individual time to teach self-help skills and toilet training. Pictures of the bathroom sequence are posted on the wall for easy reference.

Fill-ins and requests are also targeted in the restroom. Many of our students enjoy water, so a water picture is placed next to the sink for them to request the water to be turned on. Simultaneously, the adult models the manual sign for "water" to promote the request.

TIP: Do not always ask the child "What do you want?" before he requests, as this may result in the child learning to wait until you say, "What do you want?" to request, thus promoting prompt dependency. Instead, show desired items and encourage the child to initiate requests more spontaneously.

At times, it is difficult to transition students from preferred activities to the bathroom. For example, Andy's favorite activity in the classroom was playing with the tool bench. After being shown a picture and asked to go to the bathroom, Andy clung to the tool bench.

Visual bathroom schedule with sequential steps is used to promote independence.

Instead of picking up Andy, we picked up the tool bench and put it in the bathroom. All of a sudden, Andy was extremely motivated to go to the bathroom. Success!

Use reinforcers over picking up a child to take him to a given area. This will save your back and – better yet – encourage the child to be more independent and compliant.

10:30-10:45; 10:45-11:00 a.m. – Small-Group Instruction
As the children complete their bathroom breaks, they rotate through two additional adult-directed instructional settings.

11:00-11:20 a.m. – Large-Group Activity
Large-group activities include cooking, science experiments, and sensory activities targeting functional skills such as requesting, following directions, identifying and labeling vocabulary, sequencing, and fine-motor skills.

Visual pudding recipe.

Cooking Activities
Children prepare snacks such as pudding, cookies, trail mix, and other food that is related to the curriculum theme. For instance, when the students learn about movies, pop popcorn in a see-through popcorn maker for the cooking activity. The students participate by pouring the oil and the popcorn kernels into the maker. When the popcorn begins to pop, present the picture of popcorn while signing and saying "pop, pop, pop!" The students are encouraged to request popcorn during snack using the recently modeled words, manual signs, and pictures for popcorn.

In another session, the students made pudding. They followed the recipe above, which taught them how to follow directions, sequence, pour items into a bowl, and mix the pudding.

Ben taking his turn stirring the pudding.

26

Science Experiments

The children enjoy interactive science experiments, including a "volcano" made out of a water bottle, vinegar, and baking soda; goop made from corn starch, water, and food coloring; and an "ocean" in a bottle, using water, oil, and food coloring. Use duct tape to secure the top of a bottle to avoid any spills and prevent a child from "drinking" the science experiment.

Visual recipe for Ocean in a Bottle.

John and Dylan watching the "volcano" explode. Note the level of student engagement.

Volcano visual recipe.

Sensory Activities

During classroom activities, we present various sensory items, including water, shaving cream, and sand. To encourage play and minimize messes, we place a small amount of the sensory item in a plastic bin. We use bins that two children share to target children tolerating peers being close to them and playing with similar materials.

If a child avoids touching a sensory item, favorite toys are added to the material to promote acceptance. For example, Sam did not like the feel of shaving cream on his hands. If it happened, he immediately cried and tried to push away from the table. Sam loved trains, so we placed a train in a small amount of shaving cream. Suddenly having shaving cream on his hands wasn't so bad when he was able to play with his train. In this way, we were able to desensitize Sam to the shaving cream and increase the repertoire of items he would play with in the classroom.

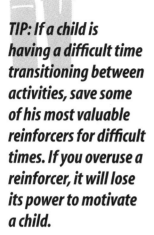

TIP: *If a child is having a difficult time transitioning between activities, save some of his most valuable reinforcers for difficult times. If you overuse a reinforcer, it will lose its power to motivate a child.*

REFLECTION: *How effective is your current classroom schedule? How can you modify your classroom schedule to meet the needs of your students?*

11:20-11:30 a.m. – Departure

The day concludes with children's self-help skills being addressed as they put on their coats and backpacks. Depending on individual needs, the students are prompted by verbal, visual, gestural and/or physical proximity of adults to locate their personal items in their cubbies. Each cubby is labeled with the child's name and picture. They are taught to put on their coats independently by placing the coat on the table or floor with the hood facing toward the child. The child inserts his arms and flips the coat over his head. We typically have to engage the zipper but encourage the children to complete the zipping.

At the end of the day, some of our students love to get on the bus while others want to stay at school. Grace was one of those who wanted to stay at school. One of her reinforcers was bubbles. We would save the bubbles for the end of the day to help her transition to the bus. One adult would walk backwards blowing bubbles as another adult held Grace's hand as they walked to the bus.

Adapting the CCSP

The CCSP is adaptable for students of various ages. Although it was originally designed as a self-contained special education program, the techniques and strategies can be applied to other classroom and therapy settings.

Once a framework and structure is created for the students and their classroom needs, the classroom environment becomes more conducive for optimal learning opportunities. Matching the environmental demands to the child's capacity is the key to instructional success! The following chapter provides a framework to promote appropriate classroom behaviors and shape disruptive behaviors.

Shaping Behavior

Children with limited language skills often communicate through their behavior. This is such a significant area to explore that we have devoted an entire chapter to the subject of behavior. Within this chapter, you will learn how to determine the function of behaviors and how to increase positive behaviors while decreasing negative behaviors through the use of functional communication training, reinforcers, and prompting. To better understand behaviors, a child's ability to process sensory information will also be discussed. The relationship between the child and the physical environment are additional components that affect a child's behavior.

Let's begin by looking at why the child is behaving in a specific way, referred to as the *function of the behavior*. For example, a child who refuses to stay in her seat to color may be trying to (a) avoid the task or (b) seek attention. Identification of the function of the behavior will assist you in determining the strategies necessary to shape the behavior.

The appearance – or how the behavior looks – is referred to as the *form of the behavior*. Examples of form include running away, biting, hitting, dropping to the floor, or screaming. One form can take on many functions. For example a child might bite because he is trying to communicate that he is frustrated and wants you to help him, or he might bite because he is upset because another child is too close to him. It is important to determine why the child displays a certain behavior in order to understand how to shape the behavior (Skinner, 1957).

Viewing behavior as a communication tool for the child and understanding the purpose of the behavior allows us to teach the child other more appropriate ways to communicate. (Communication strategies are presented in greater detail in Chapter 3.)

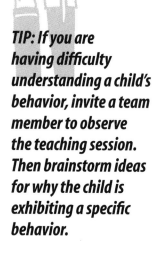

TIP: If you are having difficulty understanding a child's behavior, invite a team member to observe the teaching session. Then brainstorm ideas for why the child is exhibiting a specific behavior.

When a child is displaying appropriate behavior, remember to continue to reinforce and encourage the behavior. While reinforcers should be child-specific, always say things like "good job" or "I like how you are sitting" or exchange "high fives." These are all wonderful natural social reinforcers. Eventually the tangible reinforcers will be faded and only the social and intrinsic reinforcers remain.

Functional Behavior Assessment/ Behavior Intervention Plan

When creating a plan to replace an undesired behavior with a more positive one, it is important to collect data. This collection of information – called a *functional behavior assessment* – includes the following:

A: Antecedent – examination of what happened before the behavior was exhibited

B: Behavior – description of the form and function of the behavior

C: Consequence – examination of what happened after the incident or what consequences occurred.

By conducting a functional behavior assessment, you will see patterns and become better able to develop interventions to change or support the child's behavior. Once you understand the reason behind the child's behavior, you can teach a more appropriate way to communicate, change the child's environment, and/or change how you react to the child's behavior.

Mackenzie would frequently bite her hand. Let's analyze this behavior though the ABC:

A: The teacher was talking to another adult prior to the onset of the biting behavior.

B: Mackenzie bit her hand while looking at the adult. The *form* of the behavior was biting. The possible function of this behavior may be task avoidance or attention seeking (positive or negative).

C: The teacher stopped her conversation with the other adult and told Mackenzie "stop biting." After the teacher directed her attention to Mackenzie, Mackenzie would stop biting her hand and smile.

In analyzing the above ABC, Mackenzie's reaction immediately following the consequence indicates that she bites her hand because she obtains attention from the teacher that way. When the teacher began to give Mackenzie more attention as she displayed appropriate behaviors and ignored inappropriate behaviors, the frequency of Mackenzie's biting decreased.

By continuing to use the ABC method, you will be able to see if the changes you have made increase or decrease how often the behavior occurs. That is, by changing the antecedent and consequence, you begin to shape the child's behavior. The development of an approach to change the behavior is called *a behavior intervention plan*.

Both the functional behavior assessment and the behavior intervention plan become integral components of a child's IEP. As a child is taught more appropriate and functional means to communicate, in essence, the negative behavior decreases. The functional behavior assessment and the behavior intervention plan are reviewed and adjusted to continue to meet the child's educational needs. Thus, shaping behavior is an effective intervention that promotes learning by consistently addressing the behaviors that may be disruptive to the child's learning process.

TIP: Don't forget to make communication part of the behavior intervention for children who are nonverbal.

Functional Communication Training (FCT)

For children who are nonverbal, it is important to create a communication intervention as part of the behavior intervention plan. This is called *functional communication training* (FCT; Carr et al., 1994). FCT teaches the child another way to obtain the same outcome she obtained when she engaged in challenging behaviors. This is an "antecedent intervention" and (see page 30) must be implemented before any challenging behaviors occur.

In order for the plan to work, the appropriate behavior (communication) must yield the exact same outcome as the challenging behavior previously provided. Equally important, the challenging behavior should no longer be effective in providing that same outcome for the child. For example, if the child initially screams to get a cookie, a communication picture is created for the child to use to request the cookie. The child now gives the adult the cookie picture to request, and the screaming stops. The child uses an alternative means of communication; therefore, the outcome is the same, but the form is different. (Chapter 3 provides additional information on communication strategies.)

Reinforcers

The use of reinforcers is also an effective strategy for promoting positive behavioral changes (Skinner, 1957). A reinforcer is anything that the child finds motivating. As adults, we have our own reinforcers for completing tasks. If I asked you to hold your arm out and bend at the elbow for hours at end, would you do it? Probably not. But if I put you at a slot machine in Las Vegas, this might change things. It is much more motivating to bend your arm over and over again when you are reinforced by winning money. Children and adults can be motivated to complete various tasks with the correct reinforcer.

As we saw in Chapter 1, reinforcers take many shapes and forms. The following are reinforcers our students find motivating: spinners, ABC books, nail polish, a foot bath, receipts, magnetic letters and numbers, posters, spray candy, shaving cream, a flashlight, fruit snacks, holiday garland, markers, direct mail ads, movie figurines, a phone book, lip gloss, stickers, bubbles, a bead maze, an empty movie box, packaging from boxes, squishy balls, spinning tops, lotion, a hand held fan, hand sanitizer, a vibrating chair, an atlas, puzzle pieces, play food, a vibrating toothbrush, strings, and an artificial turf mat. Needless to say, students are motivated by a wide variety of items.

To help identify what motivate our students, we create a reinforcer inventory. We ask parents what items their child likes to hold or play with at home and also observe the child in the classroom. To add items to the child's inventory list, we present the child with a variety of reinforcers, including some of those listed above and other visual, auditory, taste, tactile, and smell stimuli. Once we have determined what a child finds motivating, we brainstorm to think of other items with similar traits the child might also find reinforcing.

TIP: Reinforcers can be tangible or non-tangible and are used as positive behavioral supports to motivate the child. Always pair a social reinforcer (e.g., high-five, "way to go!" pat on the back) with a tangible reinforcer as the use of the tangible reinforcer will eventually be faded.

TIP: Identify at least 10 items the child finds motivating. Every child is motivated by something!

The following example illustrates how we completed a reinforcer inventory.

Jacob was a 3-year-old boy who would come to school with a shoe lace in his hand. He loved to spin the string in circles. In talking to his parents, we found out that he also liked cords and wires, unfortunately these were safety hazards and could not be used.

To determine other reinforcers, we presented Jacob with a bin full of various reinforcers. He picked up a bouncy ball that was activated by pulling a string, a play camera with a strap, and our holiday garland. We had just found three more appropriate reinforcers!

When he interacted with these items, he tried to spin them like his favorite string. To expand on his interests, we thought of other items that spin, including a simple cause-and-effect toy with rotating parts, a fan, a ball drop where the balls spin down the track, and a play car ramp. Suddenly we had a variety of reinforcers we could use to shape Jacob's behaviors.

It is important to understand the power of reinforcers and the impact they have on shaping behavior. Many times, unknowingly, we reinforce the very behavior we are trying to extinguish!

Let's take an example from everyday life at the grocery store. A mother has been shopping with her child. They arrive at the check-out lane. The child sees the candy display and wants a candy bar. The child motions to the candy by reaching out with all fingers extended. The mom is busy unloading the groceries from the cart onto the counter and simply says "no." The child continues to reach and point at the candy and soon begins to scream. The mom firmly says "no" again and asks the child to be quiet, but to no avail.

The child continues to demand the candy and screams even louder. The parents gets embarrassed by the attention the screaming is getting from the other shoppers and reaches for the candy bar to give to the child to quiet him down. In doing so, the

TIP: Always be on the lookout for new reinforcers to add to the menu.

mother just inadvertently taught the child that screaming works as an effective way to communicate to get what he wants!

Prompting

Combined with reinforcers and models, prompts are powerful tools for shaping behavior and promoting learning (Skinner, 1957). The child may need to be supported in order to achieve desired behaviors in the classroom. Support is given by

- telling the child what you want him to do
- showing him what to do
- providing visual cues
- taking the child's hand to help him with an activity.

All of these are examples of the levels of prompting that are used to shape a child's behavior.

Prompts follow a hierarchy from least restrictive (verbal) to most restrictive (physical). The example below describes the use of prompts when a child is asked to clean up after playing with a toy. The hierarchy starts with the least restrictive prompt and ends with the most restrictive.

- Verbal prompt: The adult tells the child to pick up the toy.
- Visual prompt: The adult shows the child a picture representing "clean up."
- Gestural prompt: The adult points to the toy the child needs to pick up.
- Partial physical prompt: The adult lightly touches the child's hand or taps his elbow to encourage him to clean up.
- Physical prompt: The adult takes the child's hand and assists him with picking up the toy (hand-over-hand assistance).

The most natural way to prompt a child is to give a verbal request. However, other levels of prompting such as visuals, gestures, and hand-over-hand assistance may need to be added for the child to be successful at a given task. That is okay for a while, but it is important to fade prompts to prevent the child from becoming prompt-dependent.

For example, if you always say "What do you say?" before giving a child a favorite item, he will inadvertently learn that he has to

TIP: Exhaust other means of prompting before administering hand-over-hand assistance. This helps promote the child's independence.

wait for you to say this before he gets the item. In other words, he is now dependent on your verbal prompt. Vary what you say to avoid a child becoming prompt-dependent on your words. If the student is verbally prompt-dependent, talk less! Use other prompts to promote learning.

Similarly, children can become prompt-dependent on physical prompts. For example, if you always use hand-over-hand assistance to help the child turn on the faucets in the bathroom, he may wait for you to put your hand on his before turning on the water. The child is prompt-dependent on your physical help. Instead, use fewer and less intrusive prompts and fade them quickly to promote independence.

Okay, so you say: "Well, that sounds easy enough for a child who is compliant, but what about the child who dropped to the floor with a major temper tantrum the minute I asked him to do something? What if I can't get beyond the verbal prompt? What if the child has already received a reinforcer? What if he is screaming at decibels that would break your fine crystal?" What if …? What if he looks like Dylan below?

Challenging behaviors such as running away, screaming, kicking, hitting, or biting are often highly effective for getting the child something he wants or for getting him out of doing something he does not want to do. Take a deep breath and work through the behaviors by teaching the child a more acceptable way of communicating. Hang in! It may take a while, but you will get there.

Let's look at the "simple" task of teaching Dylan how to hang up his backpack.

Dylan arrived at school and entered the classroom. As part of the routine, he was asked to hang up his backpack. Dylan did not initially respond. Consequently, the adult offered him additional prompting with a picture of a backpack on the hook and using gestures by pointing to the backpack and

> **REFLECTION: Do you tend to jump in? Stop and think of whose agenda is being followed. Is it the adult's agenda to get things done within a certain length of time or the child's opportunity to learn new skills? It is often easier to complete a task for a child, but that does not teach the child. Take the time to teach the child the skills he needs to become independent with a task.**

Dylan – What now?!

then to the cubby where Dylan was to hang up his backpack. Once Dylan was asked to hang up his backpack, he stopped in his tracks, threw his backpack across the room, and dropped to the floor to assume the position for a major temper tantrum.

To start shaping Dylan's behavior, he was asked again to hang up his backpack using very few words. The adult said, "Hang up" as she presented him with visual and gestural prompts and a model. (It is recommended that you model the action using a different backpack so the child doesn't think that you have completed the task for him.)

The adult physically positioned herself behind Dylan to create a smaller teaching area, known as "tightening up" the physical environment. In other words, the child and the backpack were the only two things between the adult and the hook for the backpack.

As all these cues were given, Dylan continued to scream and kick. What Dylan wanted at this point was to do anything except hanging up his backpack. What we wanted at this point was to teach Dylan appropriate replacement behaviors to comply with the command of hanging up his backpack.

The demand of asking Dylan to pick up his backpack was repeated, but at the same time we accepted that our attempts might be unsuccessful. Next we took a deep breath and began to think about what was close at hand that could be used as an effective reinforcer (in other words, what motivated Dylan, what did Dylan value?). We tried the spinner … more screaming; we tried blowing bubbles … more kicking. Then we showed him the empty video box of his favorite movie. At this, he looked up and reached for it … ah ha … bingo! We had just found an item that Dylan valued!

By now, approximately 5 minutes had passed. Dylan had been crying non-stop and still had not picked up the backpack. We knew he was interested in the video box but would not complete the task even with this reinforcer. It was time to reassess the situation. We needed to figure out what task he could accomplish or complete.

REFLECTION: How are you and your team reacting to the challenging behaviors in your classroom? Do you believe you may inadvertently be reinforcing the wrong behaviors? If so, what is your plan to change the behaviors of the adults?

The backpack had been thrown earlier, so another adult was asked to slide it within an arm's reach of Dylan. While getting physically close to Dylan and the backpack without touching him, the adult requested that Dylan touch the backpack, while showing him the reinforcer. The verbal command continued to be given along with gestural prompts and models. Once Dylan complied and touched the backpack, he was immediately reinforced with the video box and told "Good job. You touched your backpack!" This is an example of meeting the child where he is "in the moment" and helping him to be successful. All of us get stuck, but by reducing the scope of the demand the child can still be successful.

> *Note: Within three months, Dylan was able to enter the classroom and follow a single verbal and gestural prompt to hang up his backpack. Yes! This outcome was the result of staying positive and patient, and reinforcing desired behaviors. By providing baby steps that support the child's success, in essence you have taught the foundational building blocks to get to any desired goal. This is a big elephant, and we need to eat it one bite at a time!*

When dealing with behaviors during stressful situations, stop, take a deep breath, and smile at the child. (If you are a teacher, your self-talk will be "I get paid to do this … I am not going anywhere … I can outlast you … if this is the only thing we do today, then so be it." If you are a parent, your self-talk will be "I love this child more than anything … I am not sure I can outlast you … I need to get to the bank before it closes.")

Being consistent is essential to shaping behavior. Over time, the child has learned that this behavior helps him avoid things that he doesn't want to do or that he doesn't understand. Under these new conditions, he may scream louder or kick harder because the behavior is no longer getting him what it did in the past. Stay strong, and don't give in to his escalated behaviors. Giving in only teaches the child to continue to display overt behaviors such as screaming or kicking to communicate what he wants.

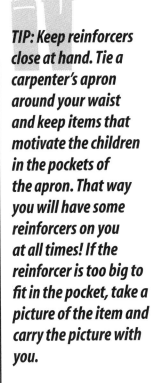

TIP: Keep reinforcers close at hand. Tie a carpenter's apron around your waist and keep items that motivate the children in the pockets of the apron. That way you will have some reinforcers on you at all times! If the reinforcer is too big to fit in the pocket, take a picture of the item and carry the picture with you.

37

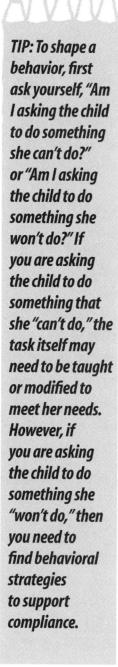

To further illustrate how to shape behaviors, let's look at the example of CJ. Happy as a lark, CJ would walk around the perimeter watching the classroom activity. The moment a demand was placed on him, he would dart in the other direction.

Our goal was for CJ to follow the schedule of the classroom activities. We began with developing a positive teaching relationship with him. As he walked around the room chewing on his stuffed toy (reinforcer), we would interrupt his walking, tell him "my turn" for the stuffed toy (his reinforcer), take the reinforcer, ask him to do a simple task (e.g., place magnetic ABCs on cookie sheet), tell him "good job," say "your turn," and then hand him back his stuffed toy (reinforcer).

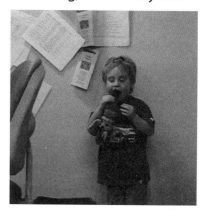

CJ with his reinforcer, walking around the perimeter of the room.

We concentrated on teaching him that first he needed to do what was asked of him, then he would receive something he wanted. We also limited the exposure he had to his "favorite" reinforcer. If we let the child have only his favorite reinforcer all day, the reinforcer itself will lose its effectiveness, and the child will be less motivated by the item.

Gradually the task transferred from standing to sitting in a chair. Over time, we moved the chair closer and closer to the table in the middle of classroom, and CJ continued to be successful. He finally discovered that sitting at the table was just as comforting as walking the perimeter of the room.

Notice above that the language of "my turn" replaces "give me." This replacement helps avoid student resistance to the trade-off and also teaches the child the beginning skills of turn taking. To warn the students of an upcoming "trade," the teacher says, "1, 2, 3 … my turn" to receive the reinforcer from the child. The reinforcer is given back to the child following completion of a desired behavior.

In addition to assessing a child's reinforcers and prompt levels, you also need to observe his sensory needs. Once you are aware of the child's sensory needs, you can imbed the necessary sensory support into his educational program, as further discussed below.

Sensory Integration

Typically, children with autism spectrum disorders have heightened sensory needs. These may range from sensory-seeking to sensory-avoiding. A child who is sensory-seeking may appear very active and enjoy activities such as climbing, jumping, bear hugs, spinning, and free falling. A child who is sensory-avoiding, on the other hand, may appear to withdraw and not like certain sounds, textures, smells, or people touching them.

A child with sensory needs may display behaviors that are easily misinterpreted as noncompliant. It is very important to observe the child and his environment to see if there are any sensory components to his behaviors, as illustrated in the following examples.

Example #1

Tommy was sensory-seeking. He would climb on top of the tables during an activity. At first when he did this it appeared as if he did not want to complete the task he was working on. However, we found that if he jumped on the trampoline 10 times before he sat at the table, he was more likely to attend to the presented task, as the jumping had a calming influence on him.

Example #2

Olivia, as opposed to Tommy, was sensory-avoiding. She would close her eyes and grind her teeth during activities. Her mother told us that she was very sensitive to fluorescent lights. So we turned off our fluorescent lights and added lamps for more natural light. This change in the environment decreased Olivia's behavior of closing her eyes and grinding her teeth.

REFLECTION: Think about your own sensory needs. When you have a headache, suddenly the typical volume of the music in the classroom may seem too loud, the lights too bright, and the smells too strong. What are the sensory needs of your students?

When a child under- or over-reacts to sensory stimulation, the child's sensory needs should be determined. Remember to talk to parents to see what is calming for the child at home and try to incorporate similar strategies at school. Also, collaborate with an occupational therapist, if available.

In addition to addressing behaviors though reinforcers, prompts, and sensory support, a relationship must be built with the child and the parent(s) to ensure an effective educational program.

Relationship with the Child

Building a positive relationship with the child is a vital component of shaping behavior (Greenspan, Wieder, & Simons, 1998). The child should want to be with you before you even start teaching. The first several days, even weeks, that a new student is in our classroom, we concentrate on pairing ourselves with the child's favorite items and activities. The goal is for the child to want to come to us. We become the holder of all that is good! While developing the relationship with the child, we also identify effective reinforcers for the child. (Chapter 4 provides additional information on how to build a relationship with a child.)

Relationship with Parent(s)

A solid teacher-parent relationship is also important for meeting the child's educational needs. Frequent communication through notes, emails, phone calls, and face-to-face visits enriches the connection between parents and teachers. (Chapter 8 provides a framework to create a parent and teacher partnership.)

Physical Environment

Behavior management also involves looking objectively at the classroom environment and modifying it to support appropriate behavior.

In the classroom, table-top activities, circle time, snack, bathroom, gross-motor, and computer stations all need to be defined areas stocked with the items/tools necessary to complete required tasks. If you have to leave the table to retrieve materials, count

REFLECTION: What is your relationship with the child's parents? Do you talk about successful/ unsuccessful strategies in the classroom and/ or at home? Do you offer parent trainings? What can you do to promote collaboration between home and school?

on the child leaving the table too, so plan ahead to prevent that from happening. (Chapter 7 provides additional information on how to set up the physical environment.)

In summary, behavior shaping is a behavior management tool used to teach effective communication and appropriate behaviors. It is important to teach the child to sit, to wait, to self-regulate, to engage, to attend to activities, and to request desired items. As educators and parents, it is our responsibility to teach the child replacement behaviors for challenging behaviors. This process can take a long time. However, by using prompts, cues, and reinforcers, you can launch the child to take the initial steps needed to reach the ultimate goals set for the child.

REFLECTION: How can you shape the behavior into a more appropriate form by redesigning your classroom? Does the physical environment reflect the flow of the classroom instruction? Is it easy for the child to transition between activities? Are you able to obtain and utilize the child's reinforcers within seconds?

Functional Communication Skills

Acritical component of the Classroom and Communication Skills Program (CCSP) is teaching children how to communicate. In this chapter, we will examine different communication modalities and ways you can support children requesting their wants and needs be met.

Some children with autism or other developmental disabilities may not be able to use spoken words to communicate. However, they are able to express their wants and needs nonverbally. This may be through an eye gaze, a slight movement, or a behavior. If a child is standing next to a desired item, he is communicating. If a child is looking up at an adult, he is communicating. If a child is screaming, he is communicating. For many children these actions take the place of words. It is up to the adults to determine what he is trying to communicate.

It is also important that we observe our own behavior. We may inadvertently be teaching the child an inappropriate way to display a behavior to get an item or reaction. For example, if the child grunts for milk and we give him milk, he has been taught that grunting leads to getting milk.

Communication intervention can replace the overt behavior – in this case grunting – by teaching the child to use words, manual signs, gestures, pictures, and/or assistive technology. That is, the behavior is replaced by a more appropriate communication form. The following example illustrates how a communication behavior was modified into functional communication.

Jack was a 4-year-old boy who loved to swing. He let us know this by jumping up and down in front of the swing and screaming. We knew what Jack wanted, but if we helped him up on the

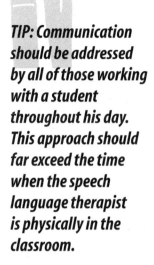

TIP: Communication should be addressed by all of those working with a student throughout his day. This approach should far exceed the time when the speech language therapist is physically in the classroom.

swing when he was screaming, he would learn that screaming equals swing. Instead, we set up the environment to encourage more functional communication. Since Jack responded well to the use of pictures, we utilized pictures as the communication system. However, we continued to present manual signs and spoken words with the pictures to promote total communication.

To begin our functional communication intervention, we Velcroed® a picture of a swing on the support bar of the swing. The teacher and speech therapist worked together. The teacher stood next to the picture while pointing to it to teach Jack how to use the picture to request. The speech therapist also pointed the picture and guided Jack towards the appropriate location.

Our first goal was for Jack to touch the picture (think baby steps!). Once he touched the picture, we put him on the swing and pushed him. After Jack was able to touch the picture independently, we increased the demand by having him give the picture to one of us as we stood next to the swing post. Next we stood a few feet away and taught Jack to bring one of us the picture. Pretty soon we were able to stand across the playground as Jack calmly walked up to one of us with a picture to request to swing.

By introducing an alternative way to communicate, we taught Jack to request desired items more functionally. A communication binder was created for Jack. Pictures of Jack's favorite items were adhered with Velcro® to pages in the book. (Photo albums may also be used to create communication binders by placing pictures in the photo pages.) The communication binder provided opportunities for Jack to request his wants and needs using pictures, all centrally located. The binder was kept with the child and sent back and forth between home and school to promote communication skills across settings. Additional pictures were added as Jack's interests in other activities expanded.

While the child who demonstrates aversive behaviors tends to get our immediate attention, the passive child is actually more difficult to teach. This is the child who sits on the swing and never fusses about not being pushed. This child may be trying to communicate with you by lifting a finger or looking at you. Or he may just sit without displaying any overt signs of intentional communication. By understanding how the child is communicating, you can shape her behaviors into more functional communication skills. In addition, note the way you are instructing. Collect data to analyze if you need to change the delivery of your instruction.

First observe the child in multiple settings and consult with the parents to determine what the child finds motivating. Often a child who is passive at school is more animated at home in a familiar setting. Once you find what is motivating, you can arrange the environment to provide opportunities for the child to request. The following example illustrates how we taught Sam to initiate functional communication.

During snack, Sam would sit patiently at the table and wait for the adult to ask him what he wanted. Through data collection (see pages 78-81), we found that Sam would only request after being asked "what do you want." He did not spontaneously initiate requests during snack time. Sam was prompt-dependent and waited until someone said "what do you want" to request.

To teach him to request a desired item spontaneously, we stopped asking "what do you want" and pointed to the picture of the cookie and signed cookie instead. One of the adults modeled how to request a cookie. She would sign, use a picture, and/or say the words. The person delivering the snack would give the other adult a part of a cookie after she requested it as a way to model requests for Sam. It was very important for us to back away from verbal prompts and talking because this was what Sam had become dependent on.

When collecting data (for further information see Chapter 6), be sure to note the level of prompting the child needs and how many times a child is requesting. We found that Sam initially was not given many opportunities to request. As a result, we changed our instruction to provide more chances for him to request in the natural environment.

TIP: *Children who are passive need to be observed very carefully to determine how they are communicating. Video taping, with parental permission, is an excellent way to watch a child more closely and repeatedly to see how the child is communicating. Watch the child to see what he reaches for, looks at, and any words, manual signs, or gestures he produces.*

TIP: Parents more or less instinctively know what their child wants. For example, if the child reaches toward the refrigerator, the adult says, "Oh, you want your milk," and gives him milk. The child learns that his needs are met without ever needing to say anything.

To teach the child functional communication skills, the parent shows the child different choices from the refrigerator. The child sees the milk and tries to say the word. He has now been taught that he has the power to get items he wants by communicating.

Teaching Communication Skills

Teach the child the power of communication. You can use a variety of communication modalities. In the CCSP, we utilize a total communication approach whereby we model manual signs, spoken words, and pictures, and use assistive devices to show the children different ways to communicate. We simultaneously embed all of these modalities into our teaching so that each child can respond using his or her preferred mode of communication.

Understandably, parents want their children to talk as soon as possible. When a child's language skills are delayed, we need to start by providing opportunities for the child to *communicate*. The first step is to set up the environment so the child learns how to functionally request. If the child's needs are met before he attempts to communicate, why would he ever need to say anything? For example, if the child typically requests to be picked up by grunting, don't react immediately. The child will probably become upset that his needs are not immediately being met. Teach the child how to request "up" by showing him the manual sign, saying the word, and/or pointing to the corresponding picture. This will help the child learn to initiate communication, not just respond to what you say (Cardon, 2007). Teaching your child how to request will increase his ability to communicate spontaneously.

Beginning communication skills should target the child's specific wants and needs. Determine the child's favorite items and teach these words first. Typically, these include toys, foods, people, and activities.

As a child learns to request, introduce other functions of language, such as choices. Present choices both verbally and visually. Be sure to vary which choice you present at the end because children with autism spectrum disorders may just repeat the last word you said, therefore not truly making a choice. Also, teach the child to fill in the blank during familiar activities such as play. For example, if a child enjoys singing "Ring-Around-The-Rosy," at the end of the song, say "all fall …" and pause to see if he can fill in "down." These activities will assist the child in developing a richer communication system.

We now explore the following communication modalities: sign language, visual supports, assistive technology, and gestures/pointing.

Sign Language

Some children have a difficult time producing speech motorically (Flanagan, 2008). Sign language is an alternative tool for teaching a child to communicate his basic wants and needs. It is nearly impossible for you to move a child's tongue, lips, and mouth to produce a meaningful sound. However, with sign language, you can shape a child's hands for him to communicate.

You can learn basic sign language through sign language vocabulary books and dictionaries (e.g., Daniels, 2001). Libraries often have manual sign language books and DVDs available for checkout. *Signing Time!* (Two Little Hands Productions LLC, 2005) is an educational video/DVD program that teaches sign language to hearing children. Manual sign language websites provide online visual dictionaries. Further, Michigan State University has a free online program that displays video clips of the manual signs for various words (http://commtechlab.msu.edu/sites/aslweb/browser.htm).

When beginning to use manual signs, it is helpful to first learn the signs for the letters of the alphabet, as these hand positions are often used to describe how to produce various vocabulary signs. Also, you do not need to sign every word. Instead, learn how to sign the words that are important to the child and to your message. For example, if you say to the child "throw the ball," sign "throw" and "ball." Remember that you are modeling communication for the child; therefore, sign the words that are functional for the child.

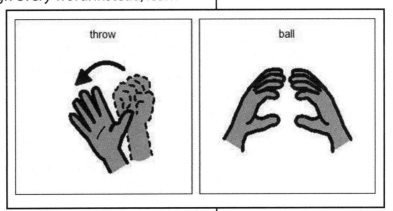

When teaching a child to communicate using manual signs, avoid teaching "more," "eat," or "please" as first signs. These words

TIP: Think about what you are teaching the child to request and make sure it is functional and appropriate for his interests.

do not provide the child with the skills necessary to request specific desired items and will lead to frustration for both the child and others around him.

To illustrate, picture a family at mealtime at a fast-food restaurant. The parent offers the child a French fry and encourages her to sign "more." The child successfully signs "more" and is given a French fry. The adult moves on to the child's drink, prompts the child to sign "more" and gives the child more to drink. Finally, the adult moves on to the chicken nuggets. The child signs "more" and is given more chicken nuggets. The adult cleans up the meal. The child approaches the adult and signs "more." The adult doesn't know what the child wants "more" of. This creates a communication breakdown that could have been avoided if manual signs representing the actual items had been taught.

As a child is learning to use manual signs, make sure that the sign he produces matches the desired item. Sometimes children offer you any and every sign they know in order to get what they want. This is called scrolling. (It looks like the hand movements of a coach on the sidelines communicating a play to players on the field.) Children with autism spectrum disorders are highly skilled at picking up patterns. If you give an item after numerous manual signs the child has produced, he may inadvertently be taught to produce a succession of signs to receive the desired item. To avoid this, if the child starts to scroll through his signs, put his hands down to "clear" the sequence. Then model and prompt the child to complete the single sign. Reinforce the child by giving him the desired item after he produces the single manual sign.

Many parents and professionals worry that if a child who is capable of learning to speak learns sign language, she will rely on that forever and will not learn to talk. However, research has shown that sign language actually helps a child speak and decreases the child's frustration by teaching communication skills (Daniels, 2001). If we rely solely on teaching a child to talk, we will miss important opportunities to teach the child to communicate. Utilizing a variety of communication modalities will help the child begin to express his wants and needs.

Visual Supports

Pictures are another effective tool to encourage a child's language learning. Pictures can be photos, pictures off product packaging, line drawings, etc. Speech and sign language are both transient – that is, the message is communicated quickly and is gone after the words have been spoken or the manual signs have been produced. Pictures and other visual supports, on the other hand, are tangible and more permanent. When following a direction provided by a picture cue, a child can continue to refer to the image to help him understand the direction. For example, if you ask the child to put something in the trash while you show him a picture of the trash can, he will be more likely to follow this direction than if the request was only given verbally.

Children can use pictures to communicate their wants and needs, but first they need to be taught what the pictures represent. That is, they need to learn the picture's meaning by association. Show the child the picture of an object as you hold the actual object next to it. This will help increase the child's understanding of what the picture represents.

Picture Exchange Communication System® (PECS; Frost & Bondy, 2004) is an effective tool to teach children to initiate communication with others. In this program, children are taught to initiate communication by giving another person a picture of a desired item. Initially, a single picture is presented to the child. The adult holds her hand out with the palm up to receive the picture. Another adult sits behind the child and prompts him to give the picture to the receiving adult. As children become more proficient, pictures are added and the children are encouraged to walk to the communication partner to request desired items. A Velcro® strip works well to keep pictures in place and allows them to be easily added, removed, or moved around.

TIP: If the child is having difficulty understanding the meaning of a picture, modify it. This may include making it larger, using only black-and-white pictures, using digital pictures or object packaging, adding texture such as a raised dried-glue border as a tactile cue, and/or placing pictures on a slant board.

Dylan requesting a "doughnut" using a picture at snack time; Grace is waiting her turn with a tangible reinforcer present.

TIP: The adults working with the child should change roles to avoid the child becoming scripted into having a specific person always lead an activity. Change roles so that children become more flexible and more likely to generalize skills.

TIP: If a child requests a cookie before dinner, it is okay to say it is not a choice. Offer the child an acceptable choice. To visually represent that an item is not available, show the child the empty box or put a red X on the picture using a dry-erase marker.

When encouraging a child to request, be sure that the desired items are out of the child's reach. If the child can easily access his favorite items, why would he need to request them from you? You can put items in a divider tray set away from the child or in plastic display boxes (found in varying sizes at craft stores) in front of the child.

When presenting a child with picture choices, be sure to also include pictures of non-preferred items. If a child is given pictures of all preferred items, she may be content with all the options and choose any picture. By providing pictures of non-preferred items, you can check how reliably the child is able to choose. Remember to give the child the non-preferred item when she requests it to teach the meaning of the pictures. It is okay to tell a child that his request is "not a choice" if it something you don't want him to have or if it is unavailable.

When presenting multiple pictures, move the pictures to different locations on the Velcro® strip to avoid the child accidentally learning to choose an item based on location, as opposed to the picture itself. In addition, check if the child understands the pictures by showing the desired item and asking him to locate the corresponding picture.

In the classroom, we placed pictures of favorite items close to the corresponding objects. This will help you quickly access the items to give to the child following his request. For example, a picture of "music" is placed directly on the CD player with Velcro®. Pictures of reinforcing toys are placed on the outside of the cabinet while the items are locked inside. This makes it easy for the child to access the picture and give it to the communication partner, thus making communication functional and more practical. The actual items still remain out of immediate reach from the child to promote requesting skills.

Assistive Technology

Assistive technology in this context refers to the use of technology to promote communication. Assistive technology can range from a single voice-output switch that delivers a message when activated to a high-tech computer that allows the user to type messages that the computer will "speak."

TIP: When using a voice output device, be sure to pair it with a visual representation of the message by placing a picture and the written word on the device.

Assistive technology use must be considered in the public school setting if it is needed for the child to receive a free and appropriate education, according the Individuals with Disabilities Education Act. As for other forms of nonverbal communication, the power of communication first needs to be taught when using assistive technology. Use a single communication voice-output switch with a programmed message and have the child activate the button to request a specific want. This teaches the child that he must initiate communication to receive a desired item or action.

Single-switch and multiple-button devices can be used during songs and activities to help the child complete fill-ins (e.g., Head, shoulders, knees, and … <u>toes!</u>; The Wheels on the bus go … *round and round*!), identify and label vocabulary, request a turn, a desired item or activity, and produce a repetitive line.

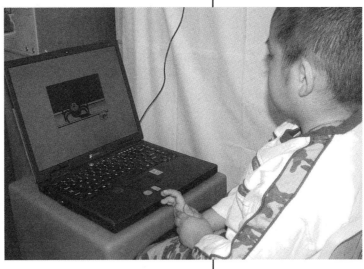

John learning how to independently activate the cause-and-effect computer software program UKanDu Switches, Too!, Eensy & Friends® (Don Johnston Incorporated) on a laptop computer.

Various alternative communication devices exist with different communication choices and access modalities. (Please see the reference list for different assistive technology devices.) Touch-screen computers and simple cause-and-effect computer programs have been used with success in the CCSP.

You can create your own cause-and-effect Microsoft PowerPoint® slide show for the students by adding text, pictures, movie clips, and sound. For example, before we went to the zoo on a field trip, we created a Microsoft PowerPoint® program in which the stu-

Functional Communication Skills

Elephant

Zoo animals – Microsoft PowerPoint® slide show sample page.

TIP: *If a child has not yet learned how to point and reaches for an object with an open hand, prompt the point by lightly pushing the outer three fingers down to isolate the index finger to create a point. Use less prompting as the child is successful to enable him to independently point to desired items.*

dents could click the mouse and see pictures of various zoo animals. Pictures were found on our local zoo website, as well as through Google™ images (http://images.google.com). We recorded our voices labeling the different animals. The children could listen to the name of the animal by pressing the speaker icon at the bottom right. This created an opportunity to incorporate technology into the program. The PowerPoint® was also e-mailed to parents to encourage the children to watch the slide show before our field trip to the zoo.

Gestures and Pointing

Children with autism spectrum disorders have difficulties understanding nonverbal language. Exaggerated gestures and pictures can help the child better understand your messages.

Children may nonverbally communicate their messages by standing next to a desired item or taking your hand to a desired item. Use this opportunity to model communication with words, pictures, and/or manual signs.

Pointing is another functional nonverbal skill that often needs to be taught. If a child wants something from the refrigerator and shows the adult what she wants by reaching towards the item with an open hand, it is unclear which items he wants. However, if the child is taught how to point, the message is delivered more clearly.

To teach a child to point, begin pointing to items you are talking with the child about. This is a great activity to do while reading a book, for example. Encourage the child to follow what you are pointing to. This is a beginning stage of joint attention (Eilan, Hoerl, McCormack, & Roessler, 2005), where the child is attending to something that you are showing him instead of only attending to his own interests. Once joint attention has been established, the child attends to your interests and you attend to his.

A typically developing child easily communicates by looking at a desired item, then at the adult, and then back at the desired item. Many children with autism and other developmental disabilities need to be directly taught this skill as they usually do not automatically pick it up on their own. By learning this skill, children realize that they can control their environment by actively engaging adults with their desires.

To encourage joint attention and eye contact, reward the child for looking at you to request a favorite item. In addition, use social praise (e.g., "high-five," hug, verbal praise) because you will eventually fade the tangible reinforcer and use more social praise. The following examples illustrate ways to teach joint attention.

CJ greatly enjoyed bubbles. To establish joint attention and reciprocal communication with CJ, we blew bubbles once and then waited. As soon as CJ looked toward us, we blew more bubbles. Soon CJ began to associate looking at the adult with bubbles. Once joint attention was established during this activity, we immediately followed through with additional communication modalities of the manual sign for bubbles and a picture cut out from the bubbles box for CJ to request bubbles in a more functional manner. He was later able to request bubbles by bringing us the picture of the bubbles, even when the bubbles were not visible.

Danny loved to swing in the bucket swing on the playground. We placed him in the swing and pulled the swing forward. Then we waited for Danny to look at us to initiate the request for us to push him on the swing. We incorporated a total communication approach for Danny to request the swing. When pushing Danny on the swing, we continued to establish joint attention with us prior to releasing the swing.

The CCSP uses a total communication approach. That is, children are exposed to sign language, pictures, spoken words, gestures, assistive technology, and written words. By providing multiple modalities, it is easier for us to determine with which modality the child is most successful. Some children gravitate towards pictures while others pick up sign language more quickly.

TIP: While eye contact is considered a desirable social behavior, do not make too big of a deal out of lack of eye contact.

TIP: Limit the number of questions you ask the child. Use more comments and descriptions instead.

Total communication should continue to be used throughout the child's program because it facilitates the child's language comprehension and use. Once the child has shown a preference for a specific communication modality, it is up to the educational team, including the parents, to determine how to continue to encourage the child's language development. In this connection it is important to remember that as adults we all use numerous modalities to communicate and that we need to teach children to do the same.

Language is not only what we say, but also what we understand. Expressive communication is the child's output, whether it is words, behaviors, sign language, pictures, or assistive technology. Receptive language is the understanding of communication and the world around the child. As educators, we must also teach a child to understand language.

Teaching Language Comprehension

When a child is beginning to speak, he says the words that are important to him or the words he has heard frequently. To help a child understand language, expose him to many different aspects of simple vocabulary. Don't just label an item. Talk about its function, where it goes, what goes with it, the category, and descriptive terms. This brings more meaning to words and brings the words to life.

> **Example:** *When playing with farm animals, instead of just saying "there's a cow," try this: "Look, the **cow** is on the **farm**. The **cow** says **moo-moo**. **Time** to **eat**, cow. He's **eating** the **grass**."*

Think of how adults learn a foreign language. If you were dropped into a foreign country where you did not know the language, you would learn the language more rapidly if people talked to you slowly and repeated key words. It would also help if others showed you corresponding items rather than asking you questions. This is an important analogy to remember when teaching children language comprehension.

As with expressive language, to encourage a child's language understanding (receptive language), use a total communication approach.

1. When giving directions, say the words, produce the signs, and show the child a picture. Keep a set of pictures on a key ring to show the child visual directions and to help her transition more easily to different activities. Take digital pictures of the child following various directions and later show her the pictures when giving the instructions.

2. Use short utterances and pause frequently to help the child become a better communicator. Give the child opportunities to use total communication to fill in the blank during favorite songs, books, or activities. For example, if the child likes to go down the slide, say, "Ready, set … (wait and let the child fill in with a word, picture, manual sign, assistive technology) … **GO**!"

    Encourage other fill-ins by pausing the music before a repetitive line in a song or waiting to say a familiar line in a book. By encouraging the child to fill in the blanks, you can build upon these skills to eventually teach your child to use these skills independently.

3. Utilize the strategies of self-talk and parallel talk, as discussed below, to assist with a student's comprehension of language.

Self-Talk

Talk about what you are doing – carry on a running dialogue of your actions. This helps to create a language connection to different things the child sees. By hearing the words over and over, the child will begin to match the words to associated actions. Use short phrases and emphasize the words that are the most important. For example, "I'm bouncing the **ball. Bounce, bounce, bounce.** Look, it's going **up**. Now **down. Up** and **down**."

Parallel Talk

This is similar to self-talk, except now you are commenting on what the child is doing. That is, attaching words to the child's

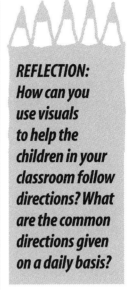

REFLECTION: *How can you use visuals to help the children in your classroom follow directions? What are the common directions given on a daily basis?*

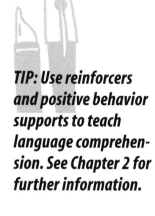

TIP: Use reinforcers and positive behavior supports to teach language comprehension. See Chapter 2 for further information.

actions. You can say the words and make the sounds the child would most likely use. Again, use short phrases and emphasize key words. For example, "**Beep**, **beep**. **Up** the ramp. **Down**, **down**, **down**. Uh-oh."

Teaching effective communication helps decrease unwanted behaviors that were previously used to communicate, creates opportunities for a child to get his needs met, allows the child to express himself, and helps the child better understand the world around him.

Communication is more than words. It includes gestures, pictures, sign language, and assistive technology. We want children to be able to communicate their desires and needs in a way that is appropriate and understandable. It is our responsibility to teach them the tools needed to become effective communicators.

Relationship Development

In order to be successful in teaching a child, the child must want to be with you. At the very heart of the Classroom and Communication Skills Program (CCSP) is the building of a relationship with each child. It is imperative to develop a trusting, caring, and fun relationship to foster the child's development.

Before School Starts

Ideally, the relationship should begin before the child's first day of school. Well before the school year starts, contact the family to set up a time for the child and the parents to come to the classroom to meet the teacher and other staff. It is important for the child to see the classroom and meet the staff to begin the transition process.

During the initial meeting, encourage the child to explore the classroom to become more comfortable in this new environment. Take digital pictures of the child, the child with the teacher, and of the teacher. Place the picture of the child on his cubby to help with identification when he starts school. Make additional copies of the child's picture to use throughout the instructional day. Also, send home a picture of yourself so the family can reference you to help prepare the child for the transition to school.

During the initial meeting(s), it is important to obtain as much information as possible from the parents. This will help you prepare the classroom environment for the arrival of the student. The following is a list of questions to help guide your conversation with parents.

- What does your child like to do at home? What are some of his favorite things? What doesn't he like? What are your child's strengths and weaknesses?
- What does your child like to eat? What foods does your child dislike? Does he have any food restrictions or allergies?

TIP: Reach out to parents and the child as early as possible before school starts to lay the groundwork for a successful transition.

- What are your child's routines at home? Do you have any safety concerns? How can we help support you at home?
- Who is in your family? Who else does your child spend time with?
- Is your child potty trained? If not, what support does he need?
- Does your child receive any outside therapy services? If so, who does he see, where does he go, and how often does he go?
- Do you have any health concerns for your child? If so, which doctors does he see? Does he take any medications or supplements?
- What would you like for your child to learn this year? What are your goals for your child?

After you have collected this information, describe the child's typical day at school. Show the parents different areas of the classroom and explain what types of activities occur during the day. To promote communication between home and school, provide a communication log or notebook including information about the child's school day as well as pertinent information from home. Also, exchange e-mail addresses and phone numbers as additional ways to contact each other.

First Day of School

For a successful first day of school, it is extremely important to have multiple reinforcers available. This will help the child's transition into the new environment. Be sure to be the first to greet the child since you are the familiar adult, assuming the recommended initial meetings have taken place. Following these recommendations will help with a smoother transition for the child. The scenarios below describe two very different first days of school.

Scenario #1 – The First Day of School … A Mismatch Between the Student and the Teacher

Teacher: (thought) Here come the buses. I guess I'll help get the students off the buses. I can't wait to greet my students and show them the way to their new classroom. We are going to have a great year!

Student: (thought) My parent just put me on a big yellow thing that moves called a bus. I don't know anyone on the bus. It stops in front of a building that doesn't look like the home I just left. A person I have never met holds out her hand to take me off of the moving thing once it stopped.

Teacher: "Hi! You must be Johnny; please hold my hand and walk with me."

Student: (thought) This is scary … there are so many kids and big people. It is getting louder by the moment. I don't really want to hold this person's hand.

Teacher: (thought) Johnny is adorable! I hope he likes his new classroom. I will show him where to put away his personal belongings. I hope he likes to play with cars and trucks.

Teacher: (thought) O.K., with a lot of assistance Johnny was able to remove his backpack and I placed it on his hook. Now let's show him the room full of cars and trucks!

Teacher: "It is time for free play … you may choose any toy to play with."

Student: (thought) She sure seems excited to show me all these things on the floor. Oh no … where did she go? I have no idea how to "play" with nor do I care to touch these things on the floor. I think I will walk around the room; I like walking around the room next to the walls. I feel safe next to the walls, away from all these new people and things. I like walking around a lot.

Teacher: "Time to clean up."

Student: (thought) I don't understand what she is asking me to do. I think I will keep walking around the room.

Teacher: Walks over to Johnny and holds his hand to guide him to help clean up. "Johnny, let's help clean up!"

Student: (thought) What in the world is this person telling me to do?! My mom always puts my stuff away … I don't think I like this place. I miss my mom! I'm going to cry!

Teacher: "O.K. everyone, it's now time for circle time!"

Student: (thought) Circle what? That was what I was doing … walking in a circle … around the room!

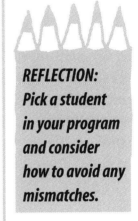

REFLECTION:
Pick a student in your program and consider how to avoid any mismatches.

59

Teacher: Walks up to the student and takes his hand. "Come on, Johnny, it's time for circle time."

Student: Stops walking, falls to the floor, and begins to kick, scream, and cry.

Scenario #2: The First Day of School ... A Match Between the Student and the Teacher

Teacher: It's the first day of school; the buses arrive. You meet the students at the buses to show them the way to their new classroom. You are looking forward to seeing Johnny and have put a few of his reinforcers in your pockets.

Student: (thought) My parent just put me on a big yellow thing that moves called a bus. I don't know anyone on the bus, but that's okay because there is a picture of my family taped to the back of the seat in front of me. The bus stops in front of a building. It looks familiar, because every day last week Mom drove me by the building. One day I got out of the car and walked around the building. Mom took a picture of me in front of the building. I have another picture of me walking inside the building and entering a classroom. I met a tall lady who smelled like peppermint. She gave me a cracker. I think she was nice. I have a picture of me, Mom, and her together – everyone is smiling. The big yellow thing stops moving, the door opens, and the tall lady who smelled like peppermint holds out her hand to take me off of the moving thing.

Teacher: "Hi! Johnny." You show the child a cracker and ask him to hold your hand. You give the child the cracker to eat along the way. "I'm glad you came to school today!"

Student: (thought) This isn't so scary. There are many kids and big people, but I am eating a cracker. I like crackers. The kids are loud. I don't like the noise ... oh, what's this? Another cracker, great! I don't really mind holding this person's hand.

Teacher: You walk the student to the classroom and show Johnny where he can put away his personal belongings. A picture of him taken a few days earlier is taped to the inside of his cubby with his name. You model how and where to put away his belongings. Once

TIP: Be honest about your own behavior and practices when striving for the "perfect" match.

Johnny has hung up his backpack, you guide him over to table full of toys and objects

Student: I like these toys. I'm not sure what to do with them. Maybe I should put them in my mouth. Hmmm.

Teacher: While observing the child's play, you model appropriate play with toys. You then give a signal/song that it is time to clean up and ask the child to put away the blocks.

Student: You mean if I put one block in the container I will get to watch the top spin (effective reinforcer)? Oh yeah! I am all over this! Now I need to put two away? Okay!

Teacher: "Everyone, it's time for circle time!" You stand in circle time with visible reinforcers.

Student: (thought) Cool! I wonder if I follow her I will get to watch the top spin again. Wow. I didn't get to see the top spin but I got to play with my favorite ball just by sitting in the chair.

Teacher: (thought) Johnny is having a great day. I am so glad he is in my classroom. We are having so much fun!

To continue to develop strong relationships with the children in your classroom, use effective reinforcers, join in the activities that the children enjoy, plan engaging lessons, and have fun. In addition, stay positive and calm with the children. This promotes a healthy learning environment. Once a solid relationship has been established with the child, you can begin to teach play skills. The following chapter provides ideas to continue relationship development through play.

TIP: When a new child is enrolled in your classroom mid-year, remember to take the time to develop the relationship – it is still the child's first day of school even if it is not the beginning of the school year.

Functional Play Skills

As children develop, play becomes the avenue through which they learn social, language, and developmental skills. Within play, a child learns to imitate, attend to others, take turns, communicate their ideas, initiate, and problem solve (Greenspan, 2006).

When you stop to think about it, play is a very complex skill. Children with autism and other developmental disabilities often need to be taught *how* to play. Observe the student and see if he is functionally playing with toys. For example, if a child is lining up the cars so they can go through the pretend car wash, this is an example of functional play. However, if the child is lining up the toys without an apparent purpose, this would not be considered functional play. The child may find comfort in the predictably in lining up the cars, but this rigid interaction with the toy does not support a purpose. We have to teach children how to play and discover that play is fun.

Strategies to Support Play Skill Development

When teaching a child the beginning stages of play, it is important to create a classroom environment that supports multiple developmental stages so you can manipulate the environment according to the child's needs. While you are teaching new play skills, the child is changing the ways she is interacting with the play item. This new way of playing for the child changes her behavior. As for any positive change of behavior, have the child's reinforcers available for immediate delivery to increase the success rate of teaching play. In many situations, you are taking the child out of her comfort zone and shaping new behaviors. Use reinforcers to assist in motivating the child.

When a child is at the beginning stages of learning how to play, use the following strategies to encourage skill development:

1. *Be animated:* Use exaggerated facial expressions and gestures to promote engagement and understanding of the play activity. Emphasize key words through manual signs, visuals, and voice animation.

2. *Use duplicate sets of toys:* By having two sets of toys, you are able to model play skills with the same materials as the child. When using your set to show the child how to play, you don't have to take the child's toy away from him or use hand-over-hand assistance.

3. *Show the child different ways to play:* Watch how the child currently plays with toys. Think of the next skills he needs to expand his play and teach him those baby steps. For example, if the child only plays with balls by rolling them back and forth, teach him to toss a ball to a partner.

4. *Interrupt the child's play:* To decrease repetitive and scripted play, interrupt the child's play sequence. For example, if the child puts a puzzle piece in the puzzle and repeatedly removes the puzzles piece and reinserts it, interrupt her play by placing your hand over the inserted puzzle piece so she cannot continue. Then show the child the next puzzle piece to put in. Once she has placed that piece, cover both pieces to prompt her to put in a third puzzle piece. Use reinforcers and praise to encourage her play.

5. *Model language:* Say and sign key words and make the sound effects your child could make during the play situation. Use fill-ins to encourage the child to complete familiar phrases.

6. *Imitate the child and encourage him to imitate you:* Play is based upon imitation. Use reinforcers to prompt the child to imitate simple motor movements with toys. Join in the child's play by imitating him and expanding his play.

By utilizing the above strategies you will be better able to support the student's play development. Start with simple toys and activities before moving into complex play. Below you will find a list of beginning toys to enrich the child's play skills.

Examples of Early Development of Play

When looking at appropriate toys for early development of play, think basic. Effective toys are those that require very little effort but offer lots of stimulating response. Examples include:

- push-and-go car
- pull-back car
- ball drop
- jack in the box
- toy that vibrates
- musical piano
- ball popper
- spiral spin top
- stacker toy with musical response
- musical shape sorter
- sound puzzles
- pop-up toy
- wind-up toy
- remote control toy
- See n' Say® (Fisher-Price)
- Sit n' Spin® (Playskool)
- balls of different sizes
- blocks
- ball mazes
- gross-motor equipment
- bubbles
- floor scooter
- water spinner
- balloon
- flashlight

This list is just the beginning. Continue to add toy selections according to the needs of the students in your classroom. Remember to follow the child's lead and observe his interests. Does he like playing with a ball, watching things fall off a table, spinning, jumping, climbing, and/or playing with puzzles? Whatever the child's interests, play along. For example, if the child likes to spin,

REFLECTION: Look objectively at the toys in your classroom. Are they developmentally appropriate? Are they exciting and engaging?

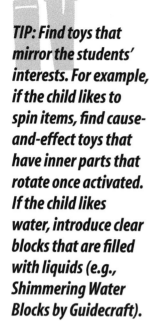

TIP: Find toys that mirror the students' interests. For example, if the child likes to spin items, find cause-and-effect toys that have inner parts that rotate once activated. If the child likes water, introduce clear blocks that are filled with liquids (e.g., Shimmering Water Blocks by Guidecraft).

pick him up and spin together or spin him by holding on to his hands. If the child likes to jump, bring out an exercise trampoline and jump with the child.

The following play examples provide ideas for continuing to build a relationship with the child, to engage the child, to promote reciprocal interactions, and to encourage play skills. Targeted concepts are listed as suggested vocabulary to use during the play activities. For many of the activities the children need the adult to assist them, increasing the use of requests and interactions with the adult.

Block Play

Set out a small pile of blocks for the child and another pile for the adult. Build a small tower and allow the child to push it over to make it crash. Next, build the tower but encourage the child to place the last block on the pile before pushing it over. Take turns placing blocks on the tower and then crashing the tower. Anticipation of watching the blocks fall now becomes reinforcing for the child.

Targeted concepts: *On, top, push, crash, big/little*

Bubble Play

Grab a bottle of bubbles, go to the center of the room, sit down, and then begin to blow bubbles … blow lots of bubbles. As the student comes over to enjoy the bubbles, keep labeling the "bubbles" or say a fill-in, "Ready, set, *BLOW*. Have pictures and assistive technology devices available to encourage the child to request "bubbles."

Targeted concepts: *bubbles, blow, pop, big/little*

Cause-and-Effect Toys

With just a push of a button or a flip of a switch, an animated toy does its song and dance. Modeling how to push the "on" switch will entice the student to keep coming back for more. Eventually, the child will be pushing the switch independently. Cause-and-effect toys are also predictable and visually stimulating, which can be motivating for children on the autism spectrum. With little effort, there is a lot of reward!

Targeted concepts: *on, off, push, pull, go, my turn, your turn*

Floor Scooters

To teach a child to move with a floor scooter, have two scooters and a rope. Sit or lie on a scooter and spin around. Ask the child to join you. If he is reluctant, provide an effective reinforcer for task compliance. Model holding onto the end of the rope and being pulled. Next, offer the rope to the child and gently pull him toward you. Other peers can be incorporated into this game by pulling and being pulled on the scooter.

Targeted concepts: *scooter, pull, spin, roll, hold, scoot, fast/slow*

Rocking Animals

Set up two rocking animals in the same play area. Encourage the children to take and wait for their turns. Say and produce the manual sign for "My turn." To teach this skill, use an effective reinforcer for compliance. Be sure to pair a social reinforcer such as a high-five with the tangible reinforcer.

Targeted concepts: *rock, stop, go, wait, my turn, your turn, sit, fast/slow*

Indoor Water Play

Fill a large plastic bin with approximately 2 inches of water and place cups and spinners in the water. Teach the children how to pour the water through the spinner. (Make sure you have plenty of towels on hand!) Have a cup available for you to model how to scoop and pour.

Targeted concepts: *water, scoop, pour, spin, go, splash, wet/dry*

Tunnels

Offer the child a tunnel to crawl through. This can be a manufactured tunnel or a large box with open ends. Join the child in the tunnel – bring along two flashlights. Play with the child by turning the flashlights on and off inside the tunnel.

Targeted concepts: *in, out, tunnel, flashlight, on, off, dark/light*

Ball Pit

Model tossing balls up in the air and letting them fall back into the pile. This is a great activity for relationship building and giggles. The ball pit is a favorite activity; however, it may be difficult to get the students out of it!

Targeted concepts: *ball, up, down, catch/throw*

TIP: Provide multiple sets of the same materials. This will allow you to model the skill you are teaching the child.

Balloons

Slowly blow up a balloon and encourage the child to request that you inflate it. You can blow up the balloon, tie it, and bounce it or you can blow up the balloon and let it go. You can also inflate a balloon by filling it with baking soda and placing it on a bottle filled part way with vinegar. The reaction between the baking soda and the vinegar will inflate the balloon.

Targeted concepts: *balloon, bounce, up/down, big/small, go, blow*

Balls

Sit on the floor with the child, roll a ball to her, and teach her to roll the ball back to you. Bounce the child on a large exercise ball while saying "bounce, bounce, bounce … stop." Teach the child to toss the ball into a large laundry basket. Incorporate reinforcers during these activities to promote participation.

Targeted concepts: *ball, roll, catch, push, my turn, your turn, bounce, go, up/down*

Outdoor Playground Equipment

Join in the fun of outdoor play. Slide down the slide with the child or if it is a double slide, slide down next to the child. Outside play is another natural environment to teach the students "fill-in" phrases. "Ready, set … *GO*" or "1, 2 … *3*, or "I want … *swing!*" Remember to wear practical clothes and shoes so you participate in outdoor play.

Targeted concepts: *slide, swing, sit, stop, go, 1, 2, 3, push, up/down*

As a child begins to develop play skills, we can continue to support him to socially interact with peers. Play is a vital component of a child's development. It is important to design programming to include supporting and teaching play skills. Play skills are the social connection to typically developing children.

REFLECTION:
What are your students' current play skills? How can you shape their play to be more functional? Are the toys in your classroom appropriate for your students?

Assessment of Student Performance

When creating a Classroom and Communication Skills Program (CCSP), it is imperative to analyze each child's performance. In this chapter, you will learn how to assess student skills, write functional goals, and monitor the progress each child is making. In the public school setting, improving student achievement and performance is mandated by federal and state laws.

An assessment in the form of measurable documentation provides teachers with students' current level of performance. From the results of the assessment, goals are developed for specific skill areas that need improvement. It is important that the goals are (a) measurable, (b) realistic considering the child's current skill level, and (c) achievable within a certain length of time. Most goals are written for a year, with benchmarks embedded as check points to ensure that they remain attainable. When adjustments of the goals need to be made, or if new goals need to be written, be sure that the decisions are data-driven (see Collecting Data, pages 78-81).

Once the child's current level of performance has been assessed and appropriate goals have been identified, data are collected to determine the child's progress towards goals. Collecting data is critical to providing factual information on the child's progress.

Data can come in different shapes and sizes, but they need to be written down or somehow recorded in a format that is meaningful and can be shared with others on the educational team, including parents.

Progress monitoring determines the child's performance and also evaluates the effectiveness of the instruction. If the data tell you that the child is progressing at the anticipated rate, continue

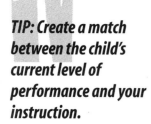

TIP: Create a match between the child's current level of performance and your instruction.

the current instructional practice. If the data are telling you that the child is not progressing or, worse, losing academic ground, change the instructional practice immediately. We strongly encourage that progress is monitored frequently. To determine a student's performance, analyze the data. Then, if necessary, adjust instructional strategies, amend the amount of time spent on a task (increase or decrease), explore other teaching materials, and check the effectiveness of the student's known reinforcers.

To improve student achievement and performance, an instructional match must be made. A match is the result of identifying the student's capacity (present level of performance) and identifying the environmental demands (what are the tasks the child is expected to complete?) and determining how closely the student skills match the difficulty of the demands placed upon her. Please see the diagram below.

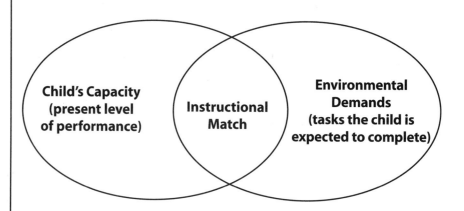

Classroom Assessments

When a student is nonverbal and/or has difficulties engaging in activities, many standard classroom assessments are inappropriate for effectively assessing the child. To decide if the assessments that you are presently using are appropriate, list the student's current level of performance in two columns. In the first column write what the student "can do," and in the second column list what the student "can't do." In order to identify and develop goals, the results of the assessment must tell you what the child "can do." It is tough, if not impossible, to write achievable goals based soley upon what a child "can't do."

We originally used a developmental checklist, which provided easy and quick monitoring of student progress. However, early on we found that we were using a simple checklist to do an extremely complex job. That is, the information we obtained from the checklist did not provide us with the information we needed to create an instructional match.

In our search for an assessment that dissected the development of skills in incremental components, we found *The Assessment of Basic Language and Learning Skills* (ABLLS; Partington & Sundberg, 1998). The focus of the ABLLS is on skill development for both communication and functional behavior, and as such it is an educational tool that combines the functions of an assessment, curriculum guide, and skill tracker. Based on information about the child's current level of performance for language and behavior development, we can manipulate the environmental demands, thereby creating a powerful instructional match.

The ABLLS divides developmental skills into 25 functional areas that, when combined, build a foundation for basic learning and communication. The 25 areas are: Cooperation and Reinforcer Effectiveness, Visual Performance, Receptive Language, Motor Imitation, Vocal Imitation, Requests, Labeling, Intraverbals, Spontaneous Vocalizations, Syntax and Grammar, Play and Leisure, Social Interaction, Group Instruction, Classroom Routines, Generalized Responding, Reading, Math, Writing, Spelling, Dressing, Eating, Grooming, Toileting, Gross-Motor Skills, and Fine-Motor Skills.

In the CCSP we use the modified version of the ABLLS assessment, which encompasses the early learner skills. The early learner skills incorporate 11 of the 25 skills identified above.

1. ***Cooperation and Reinforcer Effectiveness***: The effectiveness of reinforcers and the child's cooperation level
2. ***Visual Performance***: Matching, sorting, sequencing skills
3. ***Receptive Language***: Language comprehension
4. ***Imitation***: Imitating movements with objects, fine- and gross-motor imitation
5. ***Verbal Imitation***: Imitating speech
6. ***Requests:*** Form of the child's requests

71

7. ***Labeling:*** Naming items
8. ***Intraverbals***: Fill-ins
9. ***Spontaneous Vocalizations***: Spontaneous use of language
10. ***Play and Leisure***: Play skills
11. ***Social Interaction***: Interactions with peers and adults

This modified version offers task analysis in the areas that are significant for monitoring the progress of early learners. The other areas may be added once the child's skill level has increased to a level where he can do the presented tasks.

> ***Note:*** *A child's skill level in Cooperation and Reinforcer Effectiveness greatly impacts all other areas of skill development. Without effective reinforcers and cooperation, it is difficult to teach the child.*

The value of using ABLLS in the classroom is threefold. First, the assessment yields the child's present level of performance by analyzing each task and shows if there is a strong foundation. A child may have strengths in one domain and weaknesses in another. For example, a child may have strong matching skills but very limited imitation skills. It is important to look at each domain to determine what specific skills need to be taught.

Second, the assessment reveals existing skill areas. By knowing specifically where the child is functioning, the instructor is more effective and efficient in her teaching. Skills can be built upon to strengthen the child's developmental foundation.

Third, the assessment results may be used to change the delivery of instruction. This modification occurs when the child's strengths are determined by areas he excels in. For example, if a child has strong visual skills, visual cues can be incorporated to teach additional skills.

TIP: Have both school and home complete separate assessments in the same time frame. Compare the data from the two environments. Such comparison will show if the child is demonstrating a skill in one environment but not in the other. Determine what is different between the two environments and make adjustments accordingly to encourage generalization.

ABLLS can be conducted by anyone with a minimal understanding of applied behavior analysis. Teachers and school personnel, parents and family members, therapists, and medical personnel may all be involved in the collection of data. (The ABLLS is not a standardized assessment.)

Below is an example of the tracking system for Dylan. Remember the story of Dylan in Chapter 2 when he refused to hang up his backpack? On the grid, look at the skills he had in November upon arrival into the program. These skills are coded with black fill-in marks. By May, six months after enrolling in the CCSP, Dylan's skills progressed to areas marked by gray fill-in marks. His classroom behaviors directly correlated with these assessment findings.

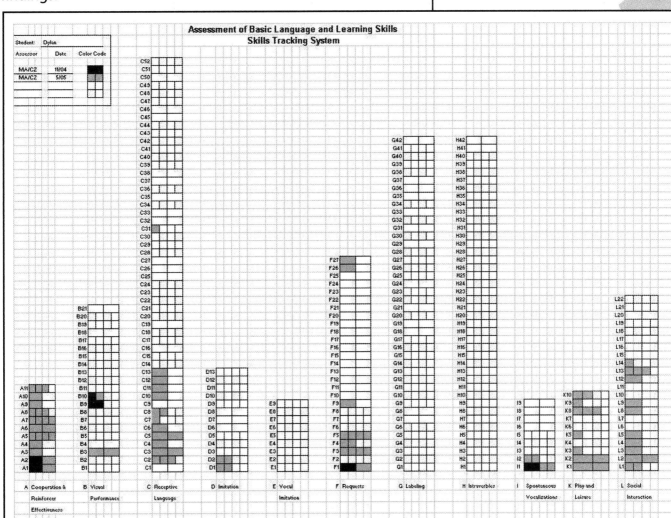

ABLLS chart demonstrating Dylan's skills in November (black) and new skills acquired in May (gray.)

Skill Areas Assessed using the ABLLS	Initial Assessment Information (November)	Second Assessment Information (May)
Cooperation and Reinforcer Effectiveness	Dylan took a reinforcer when asked some of the time.	Dylan looked at non-reinforcing items, took an offered object, responded to a variety of reinforcers, and waited for the delivery of a reinforcer.
Visual Performance	Dylan could complete four pieces of a form box and a three-piece puzzle by trial and error.	Dylan could match pictures to objects and complete a five-piece puzzle.
Receptive Language	Dylan followed simple instructions.	Dylan followed instructions to do an enjoyable activity and followed routine directions.
Imitation	Dylan was unable to imitate motor movements with objects.	Dylan imitated two actions with objects.
Verbal Imitation	Dylan was unable to imitate sounds or words upon request.	Dylan was still unable to imitate sounds or words upon request.
Requests	Dylan requested by standing next to a desired item or pulling the adult.	Dylan requested reinforcers, desired items, and actions using pictures.
Labeling	Dylan did not name reinforcing items.	Dylan continued to struggle with this task.
Intraverbals	Dylan did not fill in the blank.	Dylan continued to struggle with this task.
Spontaneous Vocalizations	Dylan babbled for at least two minutes per hour.	Dylan spontaneously said at least one word per hour.
Play and Leisure	Dylan did not actively explore toys in his environment.	Dylan played with a few toys as designed and engaged in a few appropriate outdoor play activities.
Social Interaction	Dylan demonstrated difficulties being near peers without engaging in disruptive behaviors.	Dylan responded appropriately to positive touches from peers and increased eye contact with adults.

Note: Dylan continued to make progress. He eventually was able to verbally imitate simple sounds and complete intraverbals.

Other tools and models have been developed in recent years to help assess and subsequently develop effective interventions for children with autism and other developmental disabilities. Accelerations Educational Software offers the *Discrete Trial Trainer* (Smith, 2002), a computer-based program that teaches the child various concepts as well as collects timely data for the instructor. It is easy to use and is directly aligned with the developmental hierarchy.

The *Ziggurat Model* (Aspy & Grossman, 2007) and the *Comprehensive Autism Planning System* (CAPS; Henry & Myles, 2007) are frameworks designed to match the child's needs to the appropriate intervention. The Ziggurat offers two assessment tools, the Underlying Characteristics Checklist (UCC; High-Functioning and Classic) and the ABC-Iceberg. The UCC assesses the areas of social, restricted patterns of behavior, interests, activities, communication, sensory differences, cognitive differences, motor differences, emotional vulnerability, and medical and other biological factors. The ABC-Iceberg offers illustrations of behavior patterns by gathering of data from a functional behavior assessment. Results of these assessment tools drive the interventions for the Ziggurat Model, which includes sensory differences and biological needs, reinforcement, structure and visual/tactile supports, task demands, and skills to teach.

The *Comprehensive Autism Planning System* (CAPS) is an easy-to-use system that allows educators to understand how and when to implement an instructional program for students with ASD. Specifically, it answers the questions (a) What supports does my student/child need in each class to be successful? (b) What goals is my student/child working on? and (c) Is there a thoughtful sequence to the student's/child's day that matches his learning style? Used in conjunction with the Ziggurat model, CAPS provides proactive programming in a positive format.

TIP: When writing goals, use the prompting hierarchy (see page 34) to determine the least amount of support the child needs to be successful.

Goal Development

Once an effective assessment has been completed on the child, goals are developed. Targeted goals should reflect skills the child needs to obtain. When developing goals, it is important to determine the next functional skill level to be taught.

The following is a sample list of goals that are both specific and measurable. It is up to you to determine, based upon your student's data, if they are realistic and achievable. Be sure to determine a time frame for the student to achieve the desired goal as this helps monitor the appropriateness of the goals. The following goals were created based upon the information gathered from the ABLLS, typical child development assessments, and the Foundations to the Indiana Academic Standards for Young Children from Birth to Age Five (http://www.doe.in.gov/primetime/pdf/foundations/indiana_foundations.pdf).

SKILL	GOAL
Pre-Academic Skills	• Child will track items by following the point of the instructor to various pictures in books or objects provided __(verbal, auditory) cues in x/x trials. • Child will give a single item to a teacher upon request provided __(gestural, verbal, partial physical, visual) cues in x/x trials. • Child will take a non-reinforcing item provided __(gestural, verbal, partial physical, visual) prompts in x/x trials. • Child will complete a three-piece form box when incorrect locations are covered with __% accuracy. • Child will complete a three-piece form box when given three location choices with __% accuracy. • Child will match a picture to a picture when provided with __ choices with __% accuracy. • Child will match like objects when provided with __ objects with __%accuracy. • Child will match a picture to an object when provided with __ choices with __% accuracy. • Child will complete a simple puzzle with __pieces with __% accuracy. • Child will sort __ items by color, size and/or type provided __ (gestural, verbal, partial physical, visual) prompts with __% accuracy.
Play Skills	• Child will play with __number of toys as designed for __ minutes in x/x trials. • Child will play alongside a peer without adverse reaction (i.e. list behaviors) for __ minutes in x/x trials. • Child will take turns with an adult provided __ (gestural, verbal, partial physical, visual) prompts with in x/x of trials. • Child will take turns with a peer provided __ (gestural, verbal, partial physical, visual) prompts with in x/x of trials.

Imitation Skills	• Child will imitate __motor movements provided models with __% accuracy. • Child will imitate __number of actions with a functional toy with __% accuracy. • Child will imitate __number of __(vowels, speech sounds, intonation patterns, word approximations) provided (gestural, verbal, tactile) cues with __% accuracy.
Classroom Skills	• Child will sit with a reinforcing item at a table for __minutes provided __(gestural, verbal, partial physical, visual) prompts in x/x trials. • Child will sit with a non-reinforcing item at a table __ minutes provided __(gestural, verbal, partial physical, visual) prompts in x/x trials. • Child will sit during an adult directed activity provided a reinforcer for __minutes provided __(gestural, verbal, partial physical, visual) prompts in x/x trials. • Child will sit during an adult directed activity with intermittent reinforcement for __minutes provided __ (gestural, verbal, partial physical, visual) prompts in x/x trials.
Expressive Language Skills	• Child will point to desired item provided __(gestural, verbal, partial physical, visual) prompts in x/x trials. • Child will imitate simple intonation patterns or speech sounds produced in his sound repertoire provided repeated models and reinforcers with __% accuracy. • Child will imitate __number of vowels provided repeated models, visual cues, and reinforcers with __% accuracy. • Child will imitate ___ (consonant vowel, vowel consonant, consonant vowel consonant words) provided repeated models, visual cues, tactile cues and reinforcers in x/x trials. • Child will request __number of highly reinforcing items or activities using pictures, manual signs, voice output device, and/or word approximations in x/x trials. • Child will label __number of highly reinforcing items when shown that item provided __(gestural, verbal, partial physical, visual) prompts in x/x trials. • Child will fill in the blank to complete __ number of phrases during highly motivating activities (e.g., ready, set … go) using pictures, manual signs, voice output device, and/or word approximations provided __(gestural, verbal, partial physical, visual) prompts in x/x trials. • Child will request the continuation of an enjoyable activity by using pictures, manual signs, voice output device, and/or word approximations in x/x trials provided __(gestural, verbal, partial physical, visual) prompts.
Receptive Language Skills	• Child will follow routine classroom instructions provided __(gestural, verbal, partial physical, visual) prompts in x/x trials. • Child will follow one-and two-step directions in the classroom provided ___(gestural, verbal, partial physical, visual) prompts in x/x trials. • Child will follow one-step novel directions provided ___ (gestural, verbal, partial physical, visual) prompts in x/x trials. • Child will identify __number of common objects with __ (gestural, verbal, partial physical, visual) prompts in x/x trials. • Child will identify __number of pictures of common objects with __(gestural, verbal, partial physical, visual) prompts in x/x trials. • Child will demonstrate __number of motor movement provided __(gestural, verbal, visual) cues but no models with __% accuracy. • Child will transition from one activity to another provided __(gestural, verbal, visual) cues but no models with __% accuracy.

Note: These goals should be used only as a starting point for writing student goals. Goals should be changed and worded to meet the needs of each individual student.

Collecting Data

Clear, measurable goals drive effective data collection. When designing lesson plans for an individual student and for the classroom, it is necessary to describe activities, targeted objectives, and the way skills will be assessed. Data can be collected through data sheets during a task or following an activity by using art projects, video taping, audio taping, and manipulatives and later recording this information on data collection sheets. By monitoring the child's progress, teaching effectiveness is also being monitored. If the child is not successful with a specific task, analyze how you could present and model it differently to promote understanding. It is important to record the data because if it is not written down, it did not happen!

Data Collection Sheets

Data sheets must be user friendly and easily able to monitor the child's skill level. When creating data sheets, list the targeted goal, the child's name, and the date. Data forms can be created using tables in Microsoft Word® or Microsoft Excel®. Sheets can include simple coding such as + and – or more complex coding listing levels of prompting. When creating data sheets, list the coding system on the sheet so all you have to do is to circle a behavior instead of writing out information. Data sheets can target skills for one child or for a whole class.

The following shows an example of a data sheet used for all students to assess pointing skills. By including all students' information on one sheet, the teacher spends less time flipping between pages and more time collecting data. This data sheet can be cut into student sections and stapled to individual data sheets.

Goal: Students will point to a desired item provided verbal prompts in 8/10 trials.

Date: _____

Activity: _____

Danny:	+ -	+ -	+ -	+ -	+ -	+ -	+ -	+ -	+ -	+ -	/10
CJ:	+ -	+ -	+ -	+ -	+ -	+ -	+ -	+ -	+ -	+ -	/10
Dylan:	+ -	+ -	+ -	+ -	+ -	+ -	+ -	+ -	+ -	+ -	/10
Grace:	+ -	+ -	+ -	+ -	+ -	+ -	+ -	+ -	+ -	+ -	/10
Jack:	+ -	+ -	+ -	+ -	+ -	+ -	+ -	+ -	+ -	+ -	/10
John:	+ -	+ -	+ -	+ -	+ -	+ -	+ -	+ -	+ -	+ -	/10

Additional Ways to Collect Data

The following are additional examples of how to monitor a child's progress towards written goals and classroom activity objectives:

- Use blank address labels to write quick notes about a child's performance and later place them directly on the child's goal page.

- Utilize products of typical classroom activities to collect data. For example, if the child is learning to match pictures, design an art activity to assess this skill. You can record the number of pictures the child matched along with the level of prompting the child needed directly on the back of the finished product (i.e., Matched ¾ independently, ¼ gestural prompt). This can be photocopied and saved in the child's portfolio. The following is an example of a matching art project.

Sample matching art activity – duplicate the sheet of the four pictures to the right. Leave one sheet intact and cut the other into fours.

Encourage the students to place glue on all four pictures and then have them match the pictures. Collect information related to the student's ability to match, follow one-step directions, label pictures, and/or grasp and squeeze the glue bottle.

Community Helper Vehicles

- Take auditory "notes" of the student's performance by using a hand-held digital or tape voice recorder. For example, you can record a child's level of performance on a specific task (i.e., % accuracy) and level of prompts needed. At the end of the day, transcribe the data. This provides an opportunity for data collection without having to write down information during the task.

TIP: Student progress is a helpful way to evaluate programming. Progress notes and data sheets must be functional and used to determine the next steps of programming. Do not take data just for the sake of taking data. Find a system that is functional for you and useful in helping the children continue to learn and maintain new skills.

- Use a handheld tally clicker or paper clips transferred from one pocket to another to track the number of times a behavior or skill occurs. The paper clips can be counted later to determine the child's accuracy on a task or how often the behavior happened.

- With parental permission, use videotaping to track performance of a child's skill and to evaluate your teaching. Often, after looking at a video, we observed communication attempts and skills we did not see during the original teaching session. Videotaping allows you to take a step back and truly observe your own skills and the child's skills to determine if you have created an instructional match for the student (see page 70).

- Remind staff of each student's targeted areas of skill development by placing posters on the walls listing current goals for quick reference.

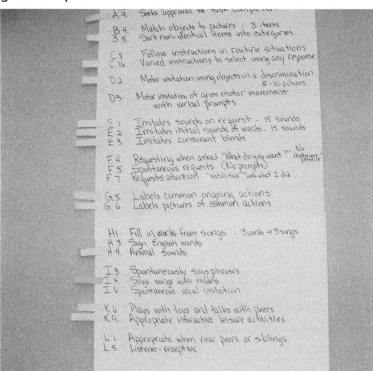

A child's specific targeted skills from the ABLLS assessment.

- Place each child's goals on different clipboards around the classroom. This allows the adults to take data in various settings without having to search for a data clipboard. Keep clipboards on hooks in the classroom.

- Include data collection sheets with instructional materials for ease of access during activities.

- Encourage the instructional assistant in the classroom to also take data. This will provide more information about the student's current skills.

Once you have collected data, it is critical to analyze it to determine the student's progress.

Progress Monitoring

Progress monitoring supports a student's learning. To implement progress monitoring, the data are analyzed to determine the child's skill level. The child's progress can be charted using Microsoft Excel® to produce graphs reflecting the child's performance. Progress toward meeting the student's goals is measured by comparing expected and actual rates of learning. Based on these measurements, teaching is adjusted as needed to meet the individual student learning needs.

In the CCSP, the student's academic performance is monitored on a regular basis. Progress reports on the student's IEP goals and objectives are sent home every nine weeks, and the ABLLS assessment is completed three times per school year. In addition, narrative progress reports are sent to parents every two weeks. These notes include the emerging skills the student is demonstrating, the student's performance on various tasks, and suggestions to use at home for carry-over and generalization of the skill development.

Pulling It All Together by Design!

In summary, the main objective of the CCSP is to create an instructional match between the child's demonstrated skills and the classroom demands. Classroom assessment, goal development, data collection, and progress monitoring are threads to be interwoven into a strong but flexible instructional tool. The combination of these components will assist in laying a strong and supportive foundation for the development of new skills for your students.

> **REFLECTION:**
> *Is your data collection system functional? How can you modify your current system to make data collection more useful for monitoring progress?*

The Classroom Environment

Arrangement of the classroom environment impacts a child's success. A structured, organized classroom is more conducive to learning than a chaotic, unpredictable environment, especially for students with autism spectrum and other developmental disabilities. When assessing your classroom environment, observe the physical aspects of the space, look for natural barriers, and determine organization levels as well as environmental stimulation.

The Physical Environment

Observe the physical structure of your classroom. Where are the tables located? Where are the chairs? How accessible are the toys and the curriculum-related materials? How do you seat yourself in reference to the child?

The follow schematic shows the way we set up our classroom.

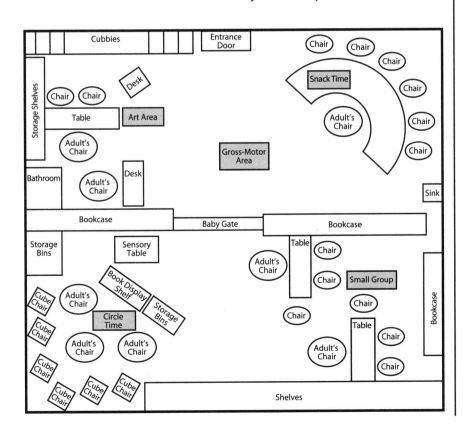

As illustrated, we placed student chairs next to walls to help create natural barriers. Bookcases and tables sectioned off areas in the classroom to create smaller learning environments. Tables for small-group instruction were placed next to bookcases and shelves for ease of accessing instructional materials. Further, the classroom was sectioned into two main parts using bookcases and a baby gate. This decreased the likelihood of the students running from one end of the classroom to the other end or leaving the classroom from the front door.

As you create a schematic of your own classroom, start by labeling and drawing where the following permanent structures are located in the room.

Possible Permanent Structures in Your Room

- ☐ Doors
- ☐ Sink
- ☐ Bathroom
- ☐ Closet
- ☐ Shelves
- ☐ Carpet/flooring
- ☐ Cubbies

Now look at what natural barriers you can use in the classroom.

Possible Moveable Items

- ☐ Bookcases
- ☐ Room screens/room dividers
- ☐ Computer
- ☐ Tables
- ☐ Desks
- ☐ Sensory table
- ☐ Storage bins
- ☐ Curtains or drapes
- ☐ Filing cabinets
- ☐ Play kitchen
- ☐ Baby gates

Use these natural barriers to create smaller learning environments. If you encounter problems with student behaviors (e.g., climbing, running), see how you can alter the environment to help limit these behaviors.

Questions and Suggestions

- *Do students wander between activities?*
  Create distinct learning areas with clear boundaries. Use natural barriers such as bookshelves, a sensory table, and cubbies to partition off areas. Smaller classrooms within the classroom are easier to manage and limit distractions.

- *Do students run from one corner to another?*
  Use physical barriers such as movable bookcases, room screens, tables, easels, and baby gates to section off areas of the classroom. These separate areas will help support the child's learning environment by limiting open access to run. Also by creating these smaller learning environments and incorporating highly motivating activities, you increase student participation.

- *Do students get up and leave activities?*
  Place the back of the student's chair against a wall and sit in front of the child to encourage her to stay with you and the activity. If the child is completing a table-top activity and the table is located in the middle of the room, provide a barrier for the child by sitting behind her with a foot extended on either side of chair. Incorporate reinforcers into engaging activities to promote participation.

- *Do students look out the window more than they look at you?*
  Close the blinds or apply Contact™ Paper to the windows to allow light in but limit outside distractions. Look for additional distractions in the classroom and determine what can be adapted to create a more favorable learning environment. Use the structure of the room to your advantage by limiting distractions and therefore increasing participation.

TIP: If the child has difficulty sitting in one place, use masking tape or a carpet square on the floor to give him a clear boundary.

TIP: To effectively teach the child, plan ahead!

Organization

By organizing the environment and making items easily accessible, the pace of your instruction can continue by keeping students engaged for longer periods of time. Organize materials, including data sheets, pens, pictures, activity materials, and reinforcers, into bins with lids. This way the child won't have to wait as you look for materials. If you have to leave the table to go find materials, odds are the child will have left by the time you return.

Organized assessment bins.

Ways to Organize the Classroom

- ☐ Develop daily bins with materials.
- ☐ Create individual activity bins.
- ☐ Assemble assessment bins.
- ☐ Place communication pictures near or on desired items to allow the children to request more easily.
- ☐ Place communication pictures of hidden items on cabinets or on plastic bins to promote requests.
- ☐ Arrange snack cards into child-specific envelopes with extras in a drawer near the snacks.
- ☐ Organize additional pictures used in various activities in a binder.
- ☐ Label bins in a closet for easy access.

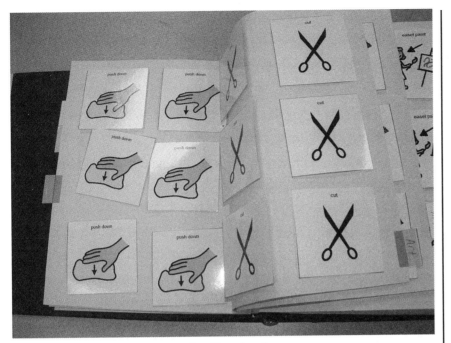

Communication pictures organized in a book.

Questions and Suggestions

- *Do students engage in inappropriate behaviors to communicate instead of using their communication systems?* Make communication systems easily accessible. Do not keep them locked away in a cabinet. Provide students numerous opportunities to communicate throughout the day by giving each student the means to communicate. For example, place pictures on a wall next to where favorite items are stored to promote requests. Create individualized communication books with pictures specific to the child that he can carry with him between activities. Place voice-output switches next to desired items so the child will have opportunities to request. Integrate communication systems into every activity.

- *Do students clear tables by dumping items onto the floor?* When placing items on a table, only put a few materials out at a time to prevent a huge clean-up. For example, if the children are playing with blocks, put out 10 blocks instead of the entire bucket of blocks. Or fill the sand table with an inch of sand instead of six inches of sand. Utilize a storage closet, larger plastic bins, or cabinets to place unused items out of sight.

TIP: If the child is learning a new communication modality, incorporate reinforcers into activities to promote its use.

TIP: Use reinforcers to encourage the child to pick up items off the floor after they have been dumped.

TIP: *Use reinforcers to encourage the child to sit in a chair.*

- *Do students leave an activity before it has started?*
  As soon as the child sits at the table, be sure everything is ready, including data sheets and instruction materials. Looking for items and trying to organize on the spot increases the likelihood that the student will leave that activity. For example, when completing an art activity, include paintbrushes, paint, paper, data sheets, pens, and reinforcers in the same bin.

The Overstimulating Environment

Observe distractions in the room. As you work with students are you competing with another item in the room that is more exciting than you are? Is there a poster, toy, or sound the child would rather attend to than you? Decrease distractions and make yourself more desirable in the classroom.

Potentially Stimulating Classroom Items

- ☐ Posters
- ☐ Decorations
- ☐ Art work
- ☐ Windows and what they reveal of the outside
- ☐ Visibility of highly reinforcing items (sink, snack items)
- ☐ Lights
- ☐ Items on a shelf
- ☐ Open sensory table

Questions and Suggestions

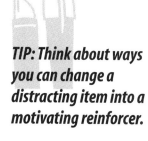

TIP: *Think about ways you can change a distracting item into a motivating reinforcer.*

- *Do students prefer to look at other items in the room rather than engaging in an activity with you?*
  Take down busy posters and use them to your advantage when you want the child to complete an activity. This is a great reinforcer that you can control. For example, when we first started, we had a large poster of cartoon characters. Jeremy would jump up and down in front of the poster. Instead of competing with the poster, we took it down and used it as a reinforcer.

  Limit distractions in the room by placing toys out of sight (a) in another room, (b) in non-see-through plastic containers, or (c) behind curtains. Shower curtains attached to shelves limit distractions and continue to provide the adults with easy access to materials. In addition, permanent structures can be blocked using a sturdy tri-fold project board (e.g., to visually block a sink).

TIP: By just making simple changes in the classroom environment, you will be able to create a more conducive learning environment. Decrease distractions in the room and spend more time teaching.

Shower curtains used as visual barriers for items placed on the shelves.

When setting up a classroom, remember to analyze the physical structure, organize teaching materials, and limit overstimulating items. Changing the environment will create more order and structure to your room. This creates a better teaching and learning environment.

Creating a Solid Parent-Teacher Partnership

A sound parent-teacher partnership is a critical component of the Classroom and Communication Skills Program (CCSP). Parents know their child best and have a wealth of information to offer about their child. Creating a positive, collaborative relationship with the parents will support the child's learning across environments.

Developing a Relationship with Parents

- Begin by incorporating the parents into the child's school programming. Invite parents into the classroom as volunteers. You can always use another set of hands! This will also provide an opportunity for you to model different behavior and communication strategies. Showing the parents how to carry out a specific approach will help them transfer this skill to the home. Develop a relationship with the parents by listening and supporting their needs.

- Based upon the needs of the parents and your students, develop and provide trainings for parents. In our classroom, we supported parents through trainings in behavior management, play skills, communication development, and understanding the IEP process. Parent trainings create additional opportunities to collaborate with parents and provide them with a network of other parents with children with special needs.

- To understand more clearly the needs of the child and the family, make a visit to the child's home. Be sure the child is home during the visit so you can see him interacting with his environment and family. Home visits yield valuable information about items and activities that are reinforcing for the child as well as continue developing a relationship with the parent and the child. The home environment provides a comfortable setting for parents to interact and problem solve with the educational team.

- Collaborate with parents to support the child's development. To encourage a child's language development at home, share communication materials with the parents. For example, if a child is using pictures to communicate at school, make multiple copies for parents, daycare providers, and grandparents. (Remember to provide the same materials to each parent in a divorce situation.) For the child using an assistive communication device, send the device to and from school, so the child will be able to use it in the home. If the child is learning manual signs at school, share with parents the signs the child is learning and using. The child will begin by producing approximations for signs. It is important to show parents how the child produces these signs so they can respond accordingly at home. In addition, teach parents positive behavioral supports and behavior management skills. This will create consistency across the child's natural environments of home and school.

Suggestions for Home

The following are ideas you can give parents to incorporate into their home and community to transfer skills the child is learning in the CCSP.

Communication

- Create choice boards using real objects or pictures for the child to use at home to select desired activities or toys. Place pictures in a scrapbook with adhesive pages or use baseball card holders to display the pictures.
- Create communication opportunities for the child with typically developing peers. Set up play dates and go to public places where there are other children the child's age.
- Try not to "talk" for the child. Allow him to respond to others using his communication modality. Encourage others to talk directly to the nonverbal child. Just because he is not talking does not mean he isn't listening!
- Let the child communicate what he wants before you meet his needs. This promotes the child's independence to communicate.
- Promote communication throughout the child's day. By deliberately not anticipating your child's every need,

TIP: Always remember that the child's parents are an integral part of the instructional team.

you create opportunities for the child to request. Limit the child's access to favorite items. If the child can open the cabinet and obtain a food item independently, why would she ever ask you for the item? Intercept the child's immediate access to items by putting locks on drawers, cabinets, and the refrigerator. Place favorite toys in sealed plastic containers. Place items up high and out of reach. Encourage your child to come to you to request items. This teaches the child the power of communication and promotes a close parent-child relationship.

- Place pictures of manual signs your child is learning at school on your refrigerator. This will help remind all family members of how to produce these signs. Remember to use manual signs for items your child enjoys. Do not use the signs "more," "please," "eat," and "thank you" for a single-word communicator because these signs are not functional. Instead, model and teach the signs that will be meaningful for the child.

- Save the packaging from toys and foods and use them as visuals for requesting.

- Create a communication book of pictures of your child's favorite items and take it with you wherever you go. This will provide opportunities for your child to express himself, regardless of the location.

- Place pictures of favorite food items on the refrigerator using magnetic tape. Lock the fridge so the child has to request his favorite foods, not just access it himself.

Language Comprehension

- When reading books with your child, face towards your child. This way, he can see your facial expressions, gestures, and manual signs while you are reading. This activity also supports joint attention.

- Take pictures of places your child visits and put them on a ring or in a photo album. Show your child a picture of the place he will be visiting before he gets into the car and allow him to hold onto it to refer to in the car. This will help with transitions and decrease anxiety of the unknown.

- Create a ring of pictures using real pictures or line drawings

TIP: By establishing ongoing communication with the child's parents, you are building the best possible program for the child.

TIP: It is hard to overdo the use of visual schedules and supports. After all, we all rely on these devices in one form or another.

to help your child follow directions. When giving your child a direction, pair it with a visual. For example, if you ask your child to get his shoes, also show him a picture of his shoes.

- Use simple schedule boards to teach your child what activities will occur during the day. Start with a single picture and gradually add pictures representing activities. Place a Velcro® strip in the car and place pictures of places the child is going to help her understand what will happen next. Instead of Velcro®, you can use a cookie sheet to mount pictures with magnetic tape. Visually, show the child the different places you will be visiting. For example, sequence a picture of the grocery store, the post office, and the park. After each place, take off the corresponding picture so the child has a visual representation of how many more places he will go to before going to the park. You can also use blank address labels to draw simple pictures of upcoming events to support transition skills. Place the stickers on her pant leg so she can refer to them easily (draw a stick picture of the child in the car and below it draw a picture of the park). Cross off each picture as the task is completed. Emphasize the concept of first and then (i.e., _first_ we need to go to the gas station, _then_ we will go to the pool). This provides visual clarity for the child.

Supporting Routines

- Make visuals that represent the sequence of daily home routines to assist the child's independence with skills (i.e., how to wash his hands, how to brush her teeth). Post these visuals in the natural place where these activities occur and refer to them while completing the skill.
- Create visual schedules at home for daily routines. For instance, use visuals to show your child the steps for getting ready for bed. There are many steps in this and other processes, so start small. Use line drawing pictures or actual photographs of the child to teach her the sequence of these skills. Independence is the goal, but we must first start teaching the individual steps to eventually obtain that goal.
- Use the dinner table to encourage functional communication skills. Model various communication modalities

and create opportunities for the child to request. Also, encourage sitting skills by incorporating a reinforcer into dinner time. Remember that the reinforcer must be something the child finds motivating at that second. If the child starts to leave the table, encourage sitting skills by using the motivating reinforcer. Start with a short amount of time for sitting and reward this behavior. You may have to start with just 30 seconds of sitting. Utilize visual timers to help your child see how much time remains for the activity. Remember, we want the child to be successful with the task. Increase the amount of time the child is expected to sit in order to reach the ultimate goal of sitting with the family during the entire meal.

Promote the Child's Learning and Play Development

- Create learning opportunities throughout the child's day. Engage your child in activities and teach him in the moment. Incorporate the child's interests into less preferred activities. For example, if your child loves water but does not like play food, put the play food in the bathtub with the child to promote acceptance.

- Involve all family members in developing of the child's skills. Families play together. Incorporate your child with a disability into that play. Teach siblings, grandparents, and friends how to encourage your child's language and interaction skills. Model ways to engage your child and teach others how they can help.

- Play with your child. Great games that children need adults to help with include bouncing high on an exercise trampoline, being swung in a swing or in a blanket, being tossed up into the air, and blowing bubbles. Incorporate a fun saying into these activities such as "Ready, set … go!" Pause before the last word to encourage your child to fill in the blank. Your child can fill in the blank using a variety of communication modalities. Remember to have fun with your child and join in with his activities.

- Reinforce sitting skills naturally in the home environment. During meal time, for example, the child can only have the desired food or drink item when he is sitting. As soon

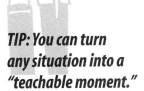

TIP: You can turn any situation into a "teachable moment."

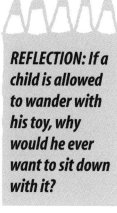

REFLECTION: *If a child is allowed to wander with his toy, why would he ever want to sit down with it?*

as the child stands up, the parent removes the food/drink item. The parent then also gives the child instructions to sit down. For example, "Sit down. I have your juice." As soon as the child sits, the parent delivers the preferred item, teaching the child that he only receives the item when seated. If the child is not motivated by food or drink, use a favorite toy as a sitting helper. If the child stands up when he has been told to sit, take the toy away and redirect him to sit down. If the reinforcer is not working, it is not effective. Try other items or activities to see what will motivate the child at that specific time.

- Analyze the child's play skills and find toys to help augment those skills. Does the child understand cause-and-effect? If not, find simple toys that will help her learn that if she activates a button, something will happen. If your child enjoys certain sensory experiences, look for toys with similar features. For example, if your child likes to watch things fall, use a ball drop toy as a functional toy that will also be motivating for your child.

Use these suggestions to help support parents as they learn to teach their children in the home environment. Learning should always be fun and functional for the child. Be a resource for parents by teaching them strategies and methods to support their child's development. By creating a strong parent-teacher partnership, you will better meet the needs of your student.

Frequently Asked Questions (FAQs)

Q: I only have one student in my school system who is non-verbal and has difficulties engaging in activities. How do I modify the CCSP to meet the students' needs within the classroom?

A: First, build a relationship with the child and motivate him to want to be with you by incorporating highly motivating reinforcers into activities. Shape the child's behavior, provide opportunities for the student to use functional communication skills, and teach sitting and attending skills. Support the child's development through the use of visual supports and a total communication approach. Incorporate activities from Chapter 1 to engage the child in learning. The Classroom and Communication Skills Program (CCSP) was created after our one student, Jeremy, entered our classroom. With the growing incidence of autism, there will likely be more students who will need the support of the CCSP in your district.

Q: Will sign language inhibit the child's ability to talk?

A: The answer is no. Children who are nonverbal are often frustrated with their inability to be understood via more traditional communication channels and, therefore, communicate through behaviors. Alternative communication modalities, including pictures, sign language, and voice output devices, provide more opportunities for the child to communicate and help decrease the child's frustration. Typically, students who start using sign language add in vocal approximations. Once the child's word approximations are more easily understood, he often drops the manual signs. Incorporating a

TIP: Look to change the way you are teaching to promote educational gains for independence!

total communication approach will help the child build the foundation for communication. If we only encourage the child to speak, we will be missing opportunities for the child to express himself and get his needs met via another avenue.

Q: **How does the CCSP teach the child to be independent, therefore, reducing the need for a one-on-one assistant?**

A: The CCSP provides the structure to create small groups and one-to-one teaching opportunities. If the child is in a teaching environment that offers strategies to learn to be independent, there is less need for the child to have a full-time assistant as support. Our goal is for the child to be independent.

Q: **How do I collect and monitor data?**

A: Data collection must be planned along with any lesson to monitor progress and make changes in programming, as necessary. Data collection sheets and other methods must be functional – quick and easy to fill out and useful in determining next goals and lesson plans. Be creative in how you collect data. Use practical tools to monitor the child's skill level, such as a clicker counter, a personal voice recorder, or paperclips transferred from one pocket to another to take data. These items can be counted and recorded after the session with the child. To determine a child's progress, use a data processing program such as Microsoft Excel® to insert data and create visual diagrams of the child's performance. This visual is easy to share with team members, parents, and administrators. See Chapter 6 for additional ideas.

Q: **How do I write appropriate goals?**

A: Writing appropriate goals can be very difficult if the assessment is not appropriate for determining the current skills of the child. To scale down the task, start by looking at the foundation skills the child needs to become successful. Can the child point? Can the child sit during an adult-directed activity? Can the child play with toys as designed? Can the child identify or name common objects? Fundamental skills must be broken down into smaller components for the child to master. (See sample Chapter 6 for helpful suggestions and sample goals.)

Q: How do you find the time to do all this?

A: How are things working for the child in the current situation? How are things working out for you? How much time is being spent "managing" behavior? When more time is spent "managing" behavior than teaching the child, something needs to change – fast! Initially, a lot of your "off hours" will be spent figuring out strategies to use, and effective ways to collect data, writing meaningful lesson plans, and setting a schedule. However, gradually, the more you immerse your new teachings into the classroom, the less the "off hours" will demand of you.

Q: How do I promote parental involvement?

A: To create a bridge between home and school, a strong partnership with parents is critical. Invite your students' parents to come into your classroom to participate as classroom volunteers. Make home visits to observe the child in his natural environment. Exchange e-mail addresses and phone numbers for quick and easy communication. Offer workshops to teach parents strategies to promote the child's learning in the home environment. Include the parents as team members when developing the child's educational program. See Chapter 8 for more information on developing a collaborative parent-teacher partnership.

Q: How do I keep the environment fun?

A: Always look to what is taught in the general education classroom and then implement the necessary modifications and adaptations to the student's curriculum in your classroom. For example, if the other children are learning about Thanksgiving in preparation for a feast, tailor the curriculum

TIP: Teach the skills necessary for the child to become independent.

REFLECTION: How are you promoting each child's independence in the classroom? What tasks are you doing for the child? How can you teach the child the skills necessary to be more independent?

TIP: Every child is motivated by something. It is your job to observe the child and consult with parents to determine which reinforcers are effective for an individual child.

to target naming common vegetables instead of focusing on pilgrims. Also, create opportunities for the students to follow a recipe to cook a dish for the feast. Remember: Fun is a huge factor when teaching a young child!

Q: How do I complete a reinforcer inventory?

A: A reinforcer inventory is imperative (see page 32). Through such an assessment, the child is exposed to multiple items as potential reinforcers and observed to see what he finds motivating. Explore all senses using smell, taste, auditory, tactile, and visual stimuli. Once a set of reinforcers have been identified, elements of those items can be used to find more reinforcing items. (See Chapter 2 for more information on completing a reinforcer inventory.) Reinforcing items change throughout a child's day. Watch the child to see what items she gravitates toward and use them as reinforcers. Continue to monitor the child. Do not allow the child continual access to reinforcing items because this will decrease its teaching effectiveness.

Q: What are some initial ideas for beginning communicators?

A: Fun activities with adults are great for beginning communicators. Start interactions with items that the child cannot operate without an adult. Bubbles are excellent. Using pictures, voice output device, sign language, or word approximations, the child can request the desired items. At first, reward attempts and then shape them into more conventional communication requests. For example, if a child is just beginning to use a picture to communicate, if he touches the picture, that action would be reinforced. As his skills improve, the criteria increase with regard to what is expected of the child to receive that item. The following are other great tools: balloons, a swing, sensory items such as shaving cream, water, and sand, pop-up toys, wind-up toys, an exercise trampoline, and a large exercise ball. Encourage communication by keeping items out of reach – in high places, locked drawers, or clear plastic bins with tight lids. Give a child small amounts of items or short turns to provide more communication opportunities.

Q: **How do I begin a conversation with my administration about starting a CCSP program?**

A: Data … Data … Data! When your data are identified and organized, they yield valuable and powerful information that shows the child's present level of performance and the direction of instruction and programming. You, along with your current data, are now ready to discuss how the CCSP will support your students' educational needs. In addition, by providing intensive early intervention that supports functional independent skills, the students will need less adult assistance, therefore decreasing the cost to the school system.

Conclusion

Thank you for examining all the endless possibilities offered by the Classroom and Communication Skills Program (CCSP) model. We encourage you to implement the CCSP into your public school setting for children with significant needs in the domains of communication, social, academic, and behavior skills.

It has been our experience that students who are nonverbal or have limited verbal skills and are in need of foundation readiness skills require a special teaching approach. Specifically, we believe that a child's educational needs are best met when addressed with a total communication approach in a natural classroom environment. By making this approach a part of early intervention, you develop and enhance the child's independent skills and facilitate his transition into a less restrictive environment.

The structure and delivery strategies used in the CCSP model lessen the need for maximum adult support and thereby prevent the problems associated with one-on-one instructional assistant proximity. These include the interference with ownership and responsibility by general educators, separation from classmates, dependence on adults, impact on peer interactions, limitations on receiving competent instruction, loss of personal control, loss of gender identity, and interference with instruction of other students (Giangreco, Edelman, Luiselli, & MacFarland, 1997).

Meeting the educational needs of the child in a natural environment is an evolving process. Within the CCSP, the child's progress is continuously assessed using appropriate assessment and monitoring tools to guide programming and ensuring it meets the child's needs.

Please remember that within each teaching session there is a natural ebb and flow. Become flexible by adjusting the time allotted and allowed for learning and task completion. Decrease or increase adult support according to the child's needs and the teaching session at hand. Assess every engagement opportunity and analyze the child's responses to the delivery of instruction. And above all, understand and use the power of receipts!

We wish you good luck in your work with young children with autism spectrum or other developmental disorders. We would love to hear from you (www.autismccsp.com).

– Megan and Colleen

Aspy, R., & Grossman, B. (2007). *The Ziggurat model: A framework for designing comprehensive interventions for individuals with high-functioning autism and Asperger Syndrome.* Shawnee Mission, KS: Autism Asperger Publishing Company.

Aspy, R., & Grossman, B. (2007). *The Ziggurat model: Underlying characteristics checklist (UCC-CL).* Shawnee Mission, KS: Autism Asperger Publishing Company.

Boardmaker® v6 (2006). [Computer Software]. Solana Beach, CA: Mayer-Johnson, LLC; www.mayer-johnson.com

Cardon, T. (2007). *Initiations and interactions: Early intervention techniques for children with autism spectrum disorders.* Shawnee Mission, KS: Autism Asperger Publishing Company.

Carr, E. G., Levin, L., McConnachie, G., Carlson, J. I., Kemp, D. C., & Smith, C. E. (1994). *Communication-based intervention for problem behavior: A user's guide for producing positive change.* Baltimore: Paul H. Brookes.

Complete Visual Support Set. (2004). Newark, DE: Pyramid Educational Products, Inc.

Daniels, M. (2001). *Dancing with words: Signing for hearing children's literacy.* Westport, CT: Bergin & Garvey.

Eilan, J., Hoerl, C., McCormack, T., & Roessler, J. (Eds.). (2005). Joint attention: *Communication and other minds: Issues in philosophy and psychology.* New York: Oxford University Press.

Flanagan, M. (2008). *Improving speech and eating skills in children with autism spectrum disorders.* Shawnee Mission, KS: Autism Asperger Publishing Company.

Frost, L., & Bondy, A. (2004). *PECS: The picture exchange system training manual* (2nd ed.). Westbury, NJ: Pyramid Educational Consultants.

Giangreco, M. F., Edelman, S. W., Luiselli, T. E., & MacFarland, S.Z.C. (1997). Helping or hovering? Effects of instructional assistant proximity on students with disabilities. *Exceptional Children, 64*(1), 7-18.

Google™ Images: Mountain View, CA: Author. Available from www.images.google.com

Greenspan, S. I. (2006) *Engaging autism: Helping children relate, communicate and think with the DIR floortime approach.* Cambridge, MA: Da Capo Press.

Greenspan. S. I., Wieder, S., & Simons, R. (1998). *The child with special needs: Encouraging intellectual and emotional growth.* Boston: Merloyd Lawrence Books.

Greg and Steve. (Release date October 14, 2003). *Brown bear, brown bear what do you see? Playing favorites.* Acton, CA: Young Heart Music.

Henry, S., & Myles, B. S. (2007). *The comprehensive autism planning system (CAPS) for individuals with Asperger Syndrome, autism, and related disabilities: Integrating best practices throughout the student's day.* Shawnee Mission, KS: Autism Asperger Publishing Company.

Indiana Department of Education and Family and Social Services Administration, Division of Family Resources, Bureau of Child Care. (Revised August, 2006). *Foundations to the Indiana Academic Standards for Young Children from Birth to Age Five.* Indianapolis: Author.

Martin, B. (1967, 1970). *Brown bear, brown bear, what do you see?* New York: Henry Holt & Company, LLC.

Microsoft Excel®. (2007). [Computer Software]. Microsoft Corporation. Redmond, WA: Author.

Microsoft PowerPoint®. (2007). [Computer Software]. Microsoft Corporation. Redmond, WA: Author.

Microsoft Publisher®. (2007). [Computer Software]. Microsoft Corporation. Redmond, WA: Author.

Microsoft Word®. (2007). [Computer Software]. Microsoft Corporation. Redmond, WA: Author.

Partington, J. W., & Sundberg, M. L. (1998). *The Assessment of Basic Language and Learning Skills (The ABLLS).* Pleasant Hill, CA: Behavior Analysts, Inc.

See 'n Say®. (2008). East Aurora, NY: Fisher-Price.

Shimmering Water Blocks. (2003-2004). Englewood, NJ: Guidecraft.

Signing Time! (2005). Midvale, UT: Two Little Hands Productions, LLC.

Sit 'n Spin®. (2008). Pawtucket, RI: Playskool, Inc.

Skinner, B. F. (1957). *Verbal behavior.* New York: Appleton-Century-Crofts.

Smith, C. (2002). *Discrete trial trainer.* Columbia, SC: Accelerations Educational Software.

Stewart, R. (Release date October 14, 2003). *Wonderful world. As time goes by, The American songbook: Volume II.* New York: J. Records.

UKanDu Switches, Too!, Eensy & Friends. (1994-1997). [Computer Software]. Volo, IL: Don Johnston, Inc.; www.donjohnston.com

Velcro®. (2007-2008). Manchester, NH: Velcro Industries B.V.

Visual Time Timer ®. (1999-2006). Cincinnati, OH: Time Timer, LLC.

Additional Resources

Anonymous. *Prompting and fading.* (2002, June). Retrieved August 12, 2002, from www.bbbautism.com/prompting_and_fading.htm

Frea, W., & Molko, R. (2004, January-February). Examining the structure of your ABA program. *Autism-Asperger's Digest, 20-25,* 48.

Furick, P. K. (2004, Feb/March). More visual supports=More expressive language. *Closing the Gap, 22*(6). Retrieved April 2, 2008, from www.closingthegap.com

Indiana Standards Tool for Alternate Reporting. (2004, October). Retrieved November 1, 2004, from www.istar.doe.state.in.us

Mesibov, G. B., Shea, V., & Schopler, E. (2004). *The TEACCH approach to autism spectrum disorders.* New York: Springer Science + Business Media, Inc.

Partington, J. W. (2006). *The Assessment of Basic Language and Learning Skills-Revised (The ABLLSTM-R).* Pleasant Hill, CA: Behavior Analysts, Inc.

Quill, K. A. (2002). *Do-Watch-Listen-Say: Social and communication intervention for children with autism.* Baltimore: Paul H. Brookes.

Assistive Technology Devices

The following are suggested assistive technology devices to be used within your Classroom and Communication Skills Program.

BIGmack® communicator
AbleNet, Inc.
2808 Fairview Avenue North
Roseville, Minnesota 55113
www.ablenetinc.com

On the Go 7 Level Communication Builder
Enabling Devices
385 Warburton Ave
Hastings-on-Hudson, New York 10706
www.enablingdevices.com

4 Compartment Communicator with Speech and Lights
Enabling Devices
385 Warburton Ave
Hastings-on-Hudson, New York 10706
www.enablingdevices.com

Cheap Talk
Novita Tech
171 Days Road
Regency Park South
Australia 5010
www.novitatech.org

Voice in a Box
Able Data
8630 Fenton Street Suite 930
Silver Spring, Maryland 20910
www.abledata.com

Talkable III with Built-in Icon Holder
Enabling Devices
385 Warburton Ave
Hastings-on-Hudson, New York 10706
www.enablingdevices.com

Talking Photo Albums
Augmentative Communication Incorporated
One Surf Way #237
Monterey, California 93940
www.augcominc.com

Talking Symbols™ Notepad
AbleNet, Inc.
2808 Fairview Avenue North
Roseville, Minnesota 55113
www.ablenetinc.com

Jelly Bean® Switch
AbleNet, Inc.
2808 Fairview Avenue North
Roseville, Minnesota 55113
www.ablenetinc.com

APC

Autism Asperger Publishing Co.
P.O. Box 23173
Shawnee Mission, Kansas 66283-0173
www.asperger.net • 913-897-1004